Robert Rose's Favorite
BEEF • PORK & LAMB

Robert
ROSE

ROBERT ROSE'S FAVORITE BEEF, PORK & LAMB

Canadian Cataloguing in Publication Data

Main entry under title:

Robert Rose's favorite beef, pork & lamb

Includes index.

ISBN 0-7788-0007-5

1. Cookery (Meat).   I. Title: Beef, pork & lamb.   II. Beef, pork and lamb.

TX749.R63 1999   641.6'6   C99-930003-2

DESIGN, EDITORIAL AND PRODUCTION: MATTHEWS COMMUNICATIONS DESIGN INC.
PHOTOGRAPHY: MARK T. SHAPIRO

We acknowledge the financial support of the Government of Canada through the Book Publishing Industry Development Program (BPIDP) for our publishing activities.
Canadä

Published by: Robert Rose Inc. • 156 Duncan Mill Road, Suite 12
Toronto, Ontario, Canada M3B 2N2 Tel: (416) 449-3535

Printed in Canada   1234567 BP 02 01 00 99

About this book

At Robert Rose, we're committed to finding imaginative and exciting ways to provide our readers with cookbooks that offer great recipes — and exceptional value. That's the thinking behind our "Robert Rose's Favorite" series.

Here we've selected over 50 favorite beef, pork and lamb recipes from a number of our bestselling full-sized cookbooks: Byron Ayanoglu's *New Vegetarian Gourmet* and *Simply Mediterranean Cooking*; Johanna Burkhard's *Comfort Food Cookbook* and *Fast & Easy Cookbook*; Andrew Chase's *Asian Bistro Cookbook*; Cinda Chavich's *Wild West Cookbook*; *New World Noodles* and *New World Chinese Cooking*, by Bill Jones and Stephen Wong; Kathleen Sloan's *Rustic Italian Cooking*; and Rose Reisman's *Light Cooking, Light Pasta, Enlightened Home Cooking* and *Light Vegetarian Cooking*.

We believe that it all adds up to great value for anyone who loves beef, pork and lamb.

Want to see more books in the series? See page 96.

Contents

Beef

Pork

Lamb

Beef

Serves 4

You can substitute pork, lamb or chicken for the beef. Just make sure to cut the meat as thinly as possible. To ensure a crunchy coating on the spring roll, the oil must be very hot. A convenient way to test the temperature is to dip a wooden chopstick into the hot oil. If it bubbles rapidly, you're all set.

Beef Tomato Garlic Spring Rolls

4 tbsp	tomato ketchup	60 mL
1 tbsp	minced garlic	15 mL
1 tbsp	*char sui* sauce *or* 2 tbsp (25 mL) barbecue sauce	15 mL
1 tbsp	rice vinegar	15 mL
1 tsp	chili sauce	5 mL
8 oz	rare roast beef, very thinly sliced	250 g
1	medium tomato, diced	1
1	green onion, thinly sliced	1
1 tsp	cornstarch	5 mL
8	egg roll wrappers	8
1	medium egg, beaten	1
1 to 2 cups	vegetable oil	250 to 500 mL

1. In a mixing bowl, combine ketchup, garlic, *char sui* or barbecue sauce, rice vinegar and chili sauce; mix well.

2. Place beef on a cutting board and cut into thin strips. Add to the sauce mixture along with tomato and green onion. Sprinkle with cornstarch and mix well. Set aside.

3. Lay 1 wrapper on a flat, dry work surface so it looks like a diamond-shaped square. Brush the outer edge with the beaten egg mixture. Place 2 tbsp (25 mL) of the filling in the center. Fold the corner of the wrapper closest to you over the filling, do the same with the sides, then roll into a tight cylinder. Repeat until all wrappers are filled.

4. In a small skillet, heat oil over medium-high heat until a strip of egg roll wrapper dropped into the oil immediately floats to the top. Add rolls in small batches and fry until golden brown, about 2 minutes per side. Drain on paper towels and keep warm until all the rolls are cooked. Transfer to a platter and serve warm.

FROM
New World Chinese Cooking
by Bill Jones and Stephen Wong

TIP

Ground chicken or veal can replace beef. Serve these burgers in a pita bun, or over half a kaiser roll.

MAKE AHEAD

Prepare beef mixture up to a day ahead and form into burgers. Freeze up to 6 weeks.

Hoisin Garlic Burgers

START BARBECUE OR PREHEAT OVEN TO 450° F (230° C)

1 lb	lean ground beef	500 g
1/4 cup	bread crumbs	50 mL
1/4 cup	chopped green onions (about 2 medium)	50 mL
3 tbsp	chopped coriander *or* parsley	45 mL
2 tbsp	hoisin sauce	25 mL
2 tsp	minced garlic	10 mL
1 tsp	minced ginger root	5 mL
1	egg	1
2 tbsp	water	25 mL
2 tbsp	hoisin sauce	25 mL
1 tsp	sesame oil	5 mL

1. In a bowl combine beef, bread crumbs, green onions, coriander, hoisin sauce, garlic, ginger and egg; mix well. Makes 4 to 5 burgers.

2. In a small bowl, whisk together water, hoisin sauce and sesame oil. Brush half of the sauce over top of the burgers.

3. Place on greased grill and barbecue, or place on rack on baking sheet and bake for 10 to 15 minutes (or until no longer pink inside). Turn patties once and brush with remaining sauce.

FROM
Rose Reisman's
Enlightened Home Cooking

Cowboy Beef Jerky

Beef jerky is a cowboy classic but it's also perfect to take along in your backpack for overnight hikes. You can also use this marinade for venison. Instead of using the oven, dry your jerky in a home dehydrator, according to the manufacturer's directions.

While you can make your own jerky, a great, preservative-free local supply can be had from Longview Meats, where Len Kirk turns out those chewy sticks you see shrinkwrapped by the till at gas stations and corner stores across Alberta. So popular and portable is the Longview Beef Jerky that local climbers hauled it up Everest during an expedition in 1994.

1 1/2 lbs	flank steak, cut along the grain into thin strips about 1/8 inch (2 mm) thick	750 g
1/2 cup	Worcestershire sauce	125 mL
1/4 cup	soya sauce	50 mL
1 tbsp	brown sugar *or* honey	15 mL
1 tsp	freshly ground black pepper	5 mL
1 tsp	seasoned salt *or* steak spice *or* seasoned meat tenderizer	5 mL
1 tsp	onion powder	5 mL
1/2 tsp	garlic powder	2 mL

1. In a zippered plastic bag, combine steak strips, Worcestershire sauce, soy sauce, brown sugar, pepper, seasoned salt, onion powder and garlic powder. Marinate overnight in the refrigerator.

2. Preheat oven to its lowest setting (about 140° F [60° C]). Lift beef strips out of the marinade; arrange on a wire rack on a baking sheet. Discard remaining marinade. Bake jerky with the oven door slightly ajar for 8 to 10 hours, turning beef strips once, or until dry and chewy. Check often; jerky should be dry but should bend without breaking. If it's brittle, you've cooked it too long for snacking but it can still be kept for rehydrating in soups and stews.

FROM
The Wild West Cookbook
by Cinda Chavich

This is a perfect meal for the Stampede party or any big summer party crowd. It can be pre-cooked the day before, then finished on the barbecue during the party. Set out some old washtubs filled with beer and ice, and serve some coleslaw and potato salad on the side. Yee-Ha!

Stampede Beef on a Bun

PREHEAT OVEN TO 300° F (150° C)
LARGE SHALLOW ROASTING PAN

1	10-lb (5 kg) beef brisket	1
	Salt and freshly ground black pepper	
1	bottle (12 oz [341 mL]) dark beer	1
1 cup	ketchup	250 mL
1/2 cup	packed brown sugar	125 mL
1	large onion, minced	1
2 tbsp	Dijon mustard	25 mL
1 tbsp	dried basil	15 mL
1 tbsp	chili powder	15 mL
1 tbsp	Worcestershire sauce	15 mL
1 tsp	liquid smoke	5 mL
3	cloves garlic, crushed	3
	Crusty onion rolls	
	Beans, coleslaw, potato salad and/or baked potatoes as accompaniments	

1. Trim brisket and roll into an evenly shaped roast, tying at intervals. Sprinkle with salt and pepper. Place in roasting pan. In a bowl, whisk together beer, ketchup, brown sugar, onion, mustard, basil, chili powder, Worcestershire sauce, liquid smoke and garlic. Pour over meat. Cover pan tightly with foil. Roast for 4 hours. Remove roast and set aside to cool slightly, reserving sauce.

2. Preheat barbecue. Grill roast over medium–low heat for 20 minutes, turning frequently, or until slightly charred and smoky. Meanwhile, bring the cooking sauce to a boil and cook to thicken.

3. Thinly slice brisket. Add to simmering barbecue sauce. Serve on crusty onion rolls, with some of the barbecue sauce.

FROM
The Wild West Cookbook
by Cinda Chavich

Serves 4

TIP

Rib eye, sirloin or tenderloin steak is great for this recipe. Chicken or pork can replace steak. Leftover cooked meat can also be used. Sauce can be used as a marinade over fish or chicken.

MAKE AHEAD

Prepare sauce up to 2 days ahead. Prepare vegetables a few hours before serving. Sauté steak just before serving and add to reheated sauce, adding a little water if the sauce thickens.

FROM
Rose Reisman's
Enlightened Home Cooking

Beef Tortillas with Crisp Vegetables and Orange Asian Sauce

PREHEAT OVEN TO 400° F (200° C)
BAKING SHEET SPRAYED WITH VEGETABLE SPRAY

2 tbsp	orange juice concentrate, thawed	25 mL
2 tbsp	hoisin sauce	25 mL
1 tbsp	rice wine vinegar	15 mL
1 tbsp	soya sauce	15 mL
1 tbsp	water	15 mL
1 tbsp	honey	15 mL
1 1/2 tsp	cornstarch	7 mL
1 tsp	sesame oil	5 mL
2 tsp	vegetable oil	10 mL
8 oz	beef steak, cut into 1/8-inch (2 mm) thick slices	250 g
1 tsp	minced garlic	5 mL
3/4 cup	chopped onions	175 mL
1 1/3 cup	chopped mushrooms	325 mL
1 1/4 cup	chopped red peppers	300 mL
1/2 cup	chopped celery	125 mL
2/3 cup	sliced water chestnuts	150 mL
1/2 cup	chopped green onions (about 4 medium)	125 mL
8	small flour tortillas	8

1. In a small bowl, whisk together orange juice concentrate, hoisin sauce, rice vinegar, soya sauce, water, honey, cornstarch and sesame oil; set aside.

2. In a nonstick skillet sprayed with vegetable spray, sauté steak until just cooked, about 1 to 2 minutes. Drain any excess liquid. Remove steak from pan. Respray skillet with vegetable spray and add oil; sauté garlic and onions until browned, about 4 minutes. Add mushrooms, red peppers and celery, and sauté for 4 minutes just until vegetables are softened.

3. Stir sauce again and add to the skillet along with water chestnuts and green onions; cook for 3 minutes or until sauce thickens. Remove from heat and stir in steak. Divide among tortillas. Roll up, place on baking sheet and bake for 5 minutes or until heated through.

Fettuccine with Beef Tenderloin, Goat Cheese and Sun-Dried Tomatoes

12 oz	fettuccine	375 g
3/4 cup	sun-dried tomatoes	175 mL
2 1/2 tsp	chopped garlic	12 mL
2 tsp	chopped ginger root	10 mL
12 oz	beef tenderloin, sliced	375 g
Sauce		
1 1/4 cups	cold beef or chicken stock	300 mL
3/4 cup	2% milk	175 mL
5 tsp	flour	25 mL
2 1/2 oz	goat cheese	60 g
1/2 cup	chopped green onions	125 mL

1. Cook the pasta in boiling water according to package instructions or until firm to the bite. Drain and place in a serving bowl.

2. Pour boiling water over sun-dried tomatoes. Let soak for 15 minutes. Drain and chop.

3. In a large nonstick skillet sprayed with vegetable spray, sauté garlic, ginger and beef just until the beef is slightly cooked, for approximately 3 minutes. Drain and remove the beef. Set aside.

4. Make the sauce: In a small bowl, combine beef stock, milk and flour until smooth; add sun-dried tomatoes and place in a skillet. Simmer until just thickened, for approximately 3 minutes, stirring constantly. Add goat cheese and reserved beef. Pour over pasta. Sprinkle with onions and toss.

FROM
Rose Reisman Brings
Home Light Pasta

Barbecued Steak with Flavored Butters

There's really nothing easier than barbecuing or broiling a good cut of beef.

Choose a tender T-bone or Porterhouse steak. A Canada Grade AAA or USDA Prime grade steak has the most intramuscular fat and will grill up the juiciest.

The best beef is well-aged — at least 14 to 21 days — and has a dark burgundy (not bright red) color. Aging breaks down some of the connective tissues in the meat, making it more tender. Supermarket meat usually sees minimal aging, so find a good butcher who knows how to handle beef.

While many people order lean tenderloin steaks in restaurants today, steak house chefs say the fattier rib eye is juicier and tastier.

FROM
The Wild West Cookbook
by Cinda Chavich

Choose a steak that's at least 3/4 inch (1.5 cm) thick for barbecuing or broiling and make sure your grill is very hot — 475 to 500° F (250 to 260° C). Sear the steak on one side, shifting it a quarter turn to get the classic cross-hatched grill marks on the meat, before turning it over to sear the second side. Douse any flare-ups with a squirt bottle of water. When the juice is starting to show on the top of the steak, it's done to perfection: medium-rare. Only a very thick steak needs to be shifted to a cooler spot on the grill and cooked longer than about 3 to 4 minutes per side. A 1-inch (2.5 cm) steak needs about 10 minutes of grill time — if the steak is 1 1/2 inches (3.5 cm) thick, grill 12 minutes. Bone-in steaks cook faster than boneless steaks.

Learn these "rules of thumb" for determining, by touch, how well your steak is done:

1. Press the triangle of flesh beneath your thumb when your hand is relaxed. It feels soft and spongy like a rare steak.

2. Touch your thumb and index finger together. Press the spot again and it will feel firmer, like a medium rare steak.

3. Touch your thumb and third finger together. Now your hand feels like a steak cooked to medium or medium well.

4. Touch your thumb to your fourth finger. The spot feels the same as a well-done steak, pretty bouncy and tough.

5. Now touch your thumb to your baby finger. The fleshy spot beneath your thumb is hard as a rock — and your steak is inedible!

Before grilling, rub the steaks with olive oil, black pepper and garlic powder or seasoning salt. A little Worcestershire sauce also makes a nice rub for T-bones.

Handle your steaks with tongs, not a fork, which will puncture the seared crust and allow the meat to dry out.

A nice addition to any barbecued steak is a compound butter; a dab melting onto a steak just as it comes off the grill.

Steak Butters

Horseradish Butter

1/3 cup	softened butter	75 mL
2	green onions, minced *or* 1/2 cup (125 mL) chopped fresh chives	2
1	clove garlic, minced	1
3 tbsp	prepared horseradish	45 mL
1 tbsp	lemon juice	15 mL
1/2 tsp	freshly ground black pepper	2 mL

Tomato Peppercorn Butter

1/3 cup	softened butter	75 mL
1 tbsp	lemon juice	15 mL
1 tsp	peppercorn mixture (black, white, green and pink), roughly crushed	5 mL
2	oil-packed sun-dried tomatoes, drained and minced	2
1	clove garlic, minced	1

Blue Cheese Butter

1/3 cup	softened butter	75 mL
2 oz	blue cheese	50 g
1 tbsp	Dijon mustard	15 mL
1 tbsp	minced shallots	15 mL
1/2 tsp	freshly ground black pepper	2 mL

1. Put ingredients for the butter you choose in a food processor and process until smooth; or, put in a bowl and combine well by hand.

2. Place the butter in dollops down the center of a piece of plastic wrap, and roll up to form a log, about 1 inch (2.5 cm) in diameter. Chill.

3. When steaks are ready, slice the butter into coins and set 1 or 2 on each grilled steak just before serving.

FROM
The Wild West Cookbook
by Cinda Chavich

Meatloaf Topped with Sautéed Vegetables and Tomato Sauce

PREHEAT OVEN TO 375° F (190° C)
9- BY 5-INCH (2 L) LOAF PAN SPRAYED WITH VEGETABLE SPRAY

Meatloaf

1 lb	lean ground beef	500 g
1	green onion, finely chopped	1
2 tsp	crushed garlic	10 mL
1	egg	1
1/3 cup	dry bread crumbs	75 mL
1 tbsp	grated Parmesan cheese	15 mL
2 tbsp	chili sauce *or* ketchup	25 mL
1/2 tsp	dried basil	2 mL
1/2 tsp	dried oregano	2 mL
1/2 cup	tomato sauce	125 mL
1 1/2 tsp	vegetable oil	7 mL
1 tsp	crushed garlic	5 mL
1/2 cup	finely diced onions	125 mL
1/2 cup	finely diced red bell pepper	125 mL
1/2 cup	thinly sliced mushrooms	125 mL
1/2 cup	tomato sauce, heated	125 mL

1. Meatloaf: In a bowl, mix together beef, onion, garlic, egg, bread crumbs, cheese, chili sauce, basil, oregano and tomato sauce until well combined. Pat into a loaf pan.

2. In a small nonstick skillet, heat oil; sauté garlic, onions, red pepper and mushrooms until softened, for about 5 minutes. Spoon over meatloaf. Bake, uncovered, for 40 to 50 minutes or until meat thermometer registers 170° F (75° C). Cover and let stand for 20 minutes before serving. Serve with tomato sauce.

FROM
Rose Reisman Brings Home
Light Cooking

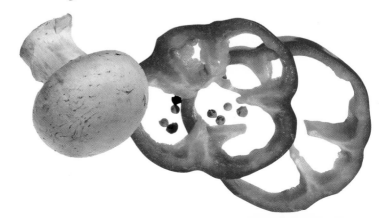

Quick Bistro-Style Steak

Serves 4

Beef is back — and that includes the mighty steak, but in well-trimmed portions. Dressed up with wine, garlic and herbs, this steak recipe becomes a special dish when you're entertaining friends.

TIP

Herbes de Provence is a blend of French herbs that often includes thyme, rosemary, basil and sage. If you can't find this blend in your supermarket, substitute a generous pinch of each of these herbs.

4	boneless striploin steaks, each 6 oz (175 g)	4
1/2 tsp	coarsely ground black pepper	2 mL
2 tsp	olive oil	10 mL
2 tsp	butter	10 mL
	Salt	
1/4 cup	finely chopped shallots	50 mL
1	large clove garlic, finely chopped	1
1/4 tsp	*herbes de Provence*	1 mL
1/3 cup	red wine *or* additional stock	75 mL
1/2 cup	beef stock	125 mL
1 tbsp	Dijon mustard	15 mL
2 tbsp	chopped parsley	25 mL

1. Remove steaks from the refrigerator 30 minutes before cooking. Season with pepper.

2. Heat a large heavy skillet over medium heat until hot; add oil and butter. Increase heat to high; brown steaks about 1 minute on each side. Reduce heat to medium; cook to desired degree of doneness. Transfer to a heated serving platter; season with salt and keep warm.

3. Add shallots, garlic and *herbes* to skillet; cook, stirring, for 1 minute. Stir in red wine; cook, scraping up any brown bits from the bottom of the pan, until the liquid has almost evaporated.

4. Stir in stock, mustard and parsley; season with salt and pepper to taste. Cook, stirring, until slightly reduced. Spoon sauce over steaks. Serve immediately.

FROM
Fast & Easy Cooking
by Johanna Burkhard

Pot Roast with Beer and Caramelized Onions

Serves 8

When I was growing up, pot roasts were a staple in my house. I can remember coming home from school to the tantalizing smell of a roast slowly braising in the oven. This recipe features a richly colored sauce from caramelized onions and a subtle sweet-sour taste from the beer and brown sugar. It's delicious served with creamy mashed potatoes or egg noodles.

TIP

Use a light-colored beer, or an amber one, such as pale ale. For a robust-flavored stew, try a dark beer, such as porter or stout.

FROM
The Comfort Food Cookbook
by Johanna Burkhard

PREHEAT OVEN TO 325° F (160° C)

3–4 lbs	beef pot roast such as cross-rib, rump or brisket	1.5–2 kg
1/4 cup	all-purpose flour	50 mL
2 tbsp	vegetable oil (approximate)	25 mL
4	medium onions, halved lengthwise and thinly sliced (about 1 1/4 lbs [625 g])	4
2 tbsp	brown sugar	25 mL
2	bay leaves	2
1 tsp	salt	5 mL
1/2 tsp	ground cinnamon	2 mL
1/2 tsp	ground ginger	2 mL
1/2 tsp	pepper	2 mL
3	large cloves garlic, finely chopped	3
2 tbsp	balsamic vinegar	25 mL
1	bottle (12 oz [341 mL]) beer	1
1	can (7 1/2 oz [213 mL]) tomato sauce	1
1 1/2 lbs	carrots (about 8)	750 g
1	small rutabaga (about 1 lb [500 g])	1

1. On a large plate, roll the meat in flour to coat. Shake off the excess; reserve.

2. In a Dutch oven, heat half of the oil over medium–high heat. Brown meat on all sides, for about 6 minutes. Transfer to a plate.

3. Reduce heat to medium. Add remaining oil to Dutch oven. Add onions, brown sugar, bay leaves, salt, cinnamon, ginger and pepper; cook, stirring often, for 12–15 minutes or until onions are softened and nicely colored. (Add more oil, if needed, to prevent onions from burning.)

4. Add reserved flour and garlic; cook, stirring, for 30 seconds. Add vinegar; cook until evaporated. Pour in beer and tomato sauce; bring to a boil, stirring, until thickened. Return meat and accumulated juices to pan. Cover and roast in preheated oven for 2 hours.

5. Meanwhile, peel carrots and rutabaga; cut into 2- by 1/2-inch (5 by 1 cm) strips. Add to beef. Cover and cook 1 to 1 1/2 hours more or until meat is tender.

6. Remove roast from pan; cut into thin slices. Arrange on a serving platter; surround with vegetables. Skim any fat from the sauce; spoon some sauce over meat and pour the rest into a warmed sauceboat to serve on the side.

Serves 4

TIP

Peel the potatoes if you like, but I find the potatoes are tastier with the skin left on.

Roasted Garlic Potatoes

PREHEAT OVEN TO 400° F (200° C)
13- BY 9-INCH (3 L) BAKING DISH, OILED

4	baking potatoes (about 2 1/4 lbs [1.125 kg]), scrubbed and cut into 1-inch (2.5 cm) chunks	4
2 tbsp	olive oil	25 mL
4	cloves garlic, slivered	4
	Salt and pepper	
1 tbsp	chopped parsley	15 mL

1. Cook the potato chunks in a large saucepan of boiling salted water for 5 minutes; drain well. Spread in baking dish. Drizzle with oil and garlic; season with salt and pepper to taste.

2. Roast for 40 minutes, stirring occasionally, until potatoes are tender and golden. Sprinkle with parsley.

FROM
Fast & Easy Cooking
by Johanna Burkhard

FROM
Rustic Italian Cooking
by Kathleen Sloan

Serves 6

This version of the classic *osso buco* is hearty, rich and red — a delicious result of the wine in which it is cooked. Serve with soft polenta.

Osso Buco
(Veal Shanks with Red Wine Sauce)

1/4 cup	olive oil	50 mL
2	onions, chopped	2
6	thick veal knuckles (*osso buco*), about 10 oz (300 g) each	6
1/4 cup	all-purpose flour	50 mL
1 1/4 cups	dry red wine	300 mL
1 cup	black olives, pitted	250 mL
1 1/2 cups	*passata* (puréed, sieved tomatoes) *or* ground tomatoes	375 mL
1 cup	beef stock	250 mL
1/2 tsp	salt	2 mL
1/4 tsp	freshly ground black pepper	1 mL
1 tbsp	grated lemon zest	15 mL
1/3 cup	chopped flat-leaf parsley	75 mL

1. In a Dutch oven or heavy casserole, heat olive oil over medium-high heat. Add onions; cook until softened, for about 5 minutes. Dust veal with flour, shaking off the excess. Brown veal on all sides, turning frequently with tongs, for about 10 minutes. Transfer to a plate.

2. Add red wine to casserole; increase heat and start scraping up any bits from the bottom and sides. Gently boil for about 3 minutes.

3. Stir in olives, tomatoes and beef stock. Add browned veal and, turning it over once or twice, bring to a gentle boil; reduce heat, cover and let cook gently for 1 1/2 hours, or until veal is tender and sauce is nicely thickened. Season to taste with salt and pepper. Serve sprinkled with lemon zest and chopped parsley.

Korean Braised Beef Short Ribs

Serves 4

Korean cuisine has its own special flavors, which rely heavily on the use of garlic, ginger, red chilies, and sesame oil. This repertoire is expanded with the judicious use of soya sauce, sweet and dry rice wines, and indigenous chili and bean pastes. These pastes are extremely complex and time-consuming to make — chili sauce, for example, requires at least 2 weeks of preparation, after which it is put out daily in the sun for 2 to 3 months! These sauces are absolutely essential to Korean cooking but, unfortunately, are quite difficult to find in North America. (Were this not so, I would have been able to include more Korean recipes.) However, here is a traditional stew that is quite easy to prepare and uses fairly common ingredients. In Korea it is made either without or with the dried chilies, so the choice is up to you.

FROM
The Asian Bistro Cookbook
by Andrew Chase

2 to 2 1/2 lbs	beef short ribs, separated	1 to 1.25 kg
3 tbsp	*sake* or 2 tbsp (25 mL) Chinese rice wine *or* dry sherry	45 mL
3 tbsp	soya sauce	45 mL
2 1/2 tbsp	*mirin* or 4 tsp (20 mL) corn syrup	35 mL
4 tsp	minced garlic	20 mL
1 tbsp	minced ginger root	15 mL
2 tsp	granulated sugar	10 mL
2 tsp	ground dried red chilies (optional)	10 mL
1 tsp	black pepper	5 mL
12	dried black mushrooms (shiitake) soaked in 1 cup (250 mL) water	12
4 tsp	vegetable oil	20 mL
Half	onion, thinly sliced	Half
1	large carrot cut into 1 1/2-inch (4 cm) cubes	1
8 oz	bamboo shoot cut into 1 1/2-inch (4 cm) pieces *or* 1 can (10 oz [284 mL]) sliced bamboo shoots, drained	250 g
8 oz	daikon radish or white turnip cut into 1 1/2-inch (4 cm) cubes	250 g
1 tbsp	*mirin* or 2 tsp (10 mL) corn syrup	15 mL
2	green onions, cut into short lengths	2
2	green finger chilies (seeded if desired), cut into short lengths	2
1/2 tsp	sesame oil	2 mL

1. In a shallow glass dish, combine beef ribs, *sake*, soya sauce, 2 1/2 tbsp (35 mL) *mirin*, garlic, ginger, sugar, pepper and ground chilies, if using. Cover; marinate at room temperature 1 to 3 hours. Drain, reserving marinade; set aside.

2. Drain mushrooms, reserving liquid. Remove and discard stems. In a skillet, heat oil over medium heat; cook mushrooms until fragrant. With a slotted spoon, remove mushrooms and set aside. Brown ribs in hot oil in 2 batches; transfer to a large saucepan. Discard any remaining oil.

3. Add to the saucepan the reserved marinade, reserved mushroom soaking liquid, onions and enough water to cover the meat. Bring to a boil; reduce heat to a simmer, cover and cook 1 1/2 hours. Add mushrooms, carrot, bamboo shoots and radish or turnip; cover and cook 20 minutes longer. Skim off the surface fat. Stir in 1 tbsp (15 mL) *mirin*; bring to a boil and cook, uncovered, until sauce reduced by half. Stir in green onions and chilies; cook 2 minutes longer. Stir in sesame oil and serve.

Serves 4

Oriental Beef Bundles in Lettuce

2 tbsp	hoisin sauce	25 mL
1 tbsp	rice wine vinegar	15 mL
2 tsp	minced garlic	10 mL
1 1/2 tsp	minced ginger root	7 mL
1 tsp	sesame oil	5 mL
12 oz	lean ground beef	375 g
1 tsp	vegetable oil	5 mL
1/3 cup	finely chopped carrots	75 mL
3/4 cup	finely chopped red or green bell peppers	175 mL
3/4 cup	finely chopped mushrooms	175 mL
1/2 cup	chopped water chestnuts	125 mL
2	green onions, chopped	2
2 tbsp	hoisin sauce	25 mL
1 tbsp	water	15 mL
8	large iceberg lettuce leaves	8

1. Sauce: In a small bowl, whisk together hoisin, vinegar, garlic, ginger and sesame oil; set aside.

2. In a nonstick skillet sprayed with vegetable spray, cook beef over medium heat for 5 minutes, or until browned; remove from skillet. Drain any excess liquid.

3. In the same skillet, heat oil over medium heat. Add carrots and cook for 3 minutes. Add red peppers and mushrooms and cook for 3 minutes or until softened. Return beef to pan along with water chestnuts and green onions. Add sauce and cook for 2 minutes.

4. Combine hoisin sauce and water in a small bowl. Place a little over the leaves. Divide beef mixture among lettuce leaves. Serve open or rolled up.

FROM
Rose Reisman's
Enlightened Home Cooking

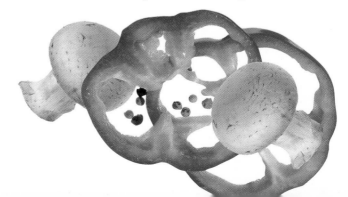

Basic Meatballs

Makes about 72 appetizers or 48 meatballs for Spaghetti and Meatballs (recipe follows)

TIP

For Spaghetti and Meatballs, follow the recipe as given but increase the size of the meatballs to 1 1/2 inches (4 cm) and lengthen the baking time to 25 minutes.

Take advantage of supermarket specials and buy lean ground beef in bulk to make batches of these tasty meatballs. Keep them in the freezer for quick appetizers or to use in pasta sauces.

Cooked meatballs can be made up to 1 day ahead and kept covered in the refrigerator, or frozen for up to 2 months. To freeze, place meatballs in a single layer on trays; when frozen, transfer to covered containers. To defrost quickly, place meatballs in a casserole dish and microwave at High for 4 to 5 minutes until just warmed through, stirring once.

PREHEAT OVEN TO 400° F (200° C)
RIMMED BAKING SHEET, GREASED

1 tbsp	vegetable oil	15 mL
1	medium onion, finely chopped	1
2	cloves garlic, minced	2
3/4 tsp	salt	4 mL
1/2 tsp	dried thyme	2 mL
1/2 tsp	pepper	2 mL
1/2 cup	beef stock	125 mL
2 tsp	Worcestershire sauce	10 mL
2 lbs	lean ground beef	1 kg
1 cup	soft bread crumbs	250 mL
2 tbsp	finely chopped fresh parsley	25 mL
1	large egg, lightly beaten	1

1. In a medium nonstick skillet, heat oil over medium heat. Add onion, garlic, salt, thyme and pepper; cook, stirring often, for 5 minutes or until softened. Stir in beef stock and Worcestershire sauce; let cool slightly.

2. In a bowl combine onion mixture, ground beef, bread crumbs, parsley and egg; mix thoroughly.

3. Form beef mixture into 1-inch (2.5 cm) balls for appetizers or 1 1/2-inch (4 cm) balls for SPAGHETTI AND MEATBALLS. Arrange on prepared baking sheet. Bake in preheated oven for 18 to 20 minutes for appetizers, 25 minutes for SPAGHETTI AND MEATBALLS, or until nicely browned. Transfer to a paper towel-lined plate to drain.

FROM
The Comfort Food Cookbook
by Johanna Burkhard

Spaghetti with Meatballs

2 tbsp	olive oil	25 mL
1	medium onion, finely chopped	1
2	medium carrots, peeled and finely chopped	2
1	stalk celery, including leaves, finely chopped	1
4	cloves garlic, finely chopped	4
1 tbsp	dried basil	15 mL
1 1/2 tsp	dried oregano	7 mL
1 tsp	salt	5 mL
1 tsp	granulated sugar	5 mL
1/2 tsp	pepper	2 mL
1	bay leaf	1
2	cans (28 oz [796 mL]) plum tomatoes, chopped	2
1	can (5 1/2 oz [156 mL]) tomato paste	1
1/4 cup	finely chopped fresh parsley	50 mL
Half	BASIC MEATBALLS (see recipe, page 31)	Half
1/2 cup	beef stock	125 mL
12 oz	cooked spaghetti or other string pasta	375 g
	Parmesan cheese	

1. In a Dutch oven, heat oil over medium-high heat. Add onion, carrots, celery, garlic, basil, oregano, salt, sugar, pepper and bay leaf; cook, stirring often, for 5 minutes or until vegetables are softened.

2. Stir in tomatoes, tomato paste and 1 tomato-paste can of water. Bring to a boil; reduce heat and simmer, par-tially covered, for 35 to 40 minutes, stirring occasional-ly, until slightly thickened. Remove the bay leaf; stir in parsley. Reserve 3 cups for Spaghetti and Meatballs. Allow the remaining sauce to cool, pack into containers and refrigerate or freeze for future use.

3. In a large saucepan, combine 3 cups (750 mL) of the tomato sauce, the meatballs and beef stock. Bring to a boil, reduce heat and simmer, covered, for 15 minutes. Toss with cooked pasta and sprinkle with Parmesan cheese.

Peppered Beef with Flat Rice Noodles

Serves 4

This Chinese version of pepper steak is one of our family favorites. For extra spice, add 2 tsp (10 mL) of satay sauce to the sauce mixture. For variety, we sometimes replace the peppers with shredded cabbage, Napa cabbage or broccoli.

Marinade

1 tbsp	oyster sauce	15 mL
1 tbsp	soya sauce	15 mL
1 tsp	coarsely ground black pepper	5 mL
2 tbsp	sherry	25 mL
1 1/2 tsp	cornstarch	7 mL
12 oz	sirloin steak, cut into thin strips	375 g

Sauce

1 tbsp	soya sauce	15 mL
1/4 cup	chicken stock	50 mL
1 lb	fresh flat rice noodles or fresh fettuccine	500 g
2 tbsp	vegetable oil	25 mL
3 tbsp	finely chopped shallots	45 mL
1 tbsp	finely chopped ginger root	15 mL
1 tbsp	finely chopped garlic	15 mL
3/4 cup	thinly sliced green bell peppers	175 mL
3/4 cup	thinly sliced red bell peppers	175 mL
1 cup	bean sprouts, packed down	250 mL
	Freshly ground pepper	

1. In a medium-sized bowl, combine ingredients for the marinade. Add beef and marinate for 20 minutes.

2. In a small bowl, prepare sauce by combining soya sauce and chicken stock; set aside.

3. If using fresh rice noodles, break them up by placing in a colander, running hot water over them and separating the strands with your fingers. (If using fettuccine, prepare according to the package directions, drain and coat with a little oil.)

4. In a nonstick wok or skillet, heat oil over high heat for 30 seconds. Add shallots, ginger root and garlic; stir-fry for 30 seconds. Add beef and stir-fry for 2 minutes, stirring to separate pieces. Add peppers and stir-fry for 2 minutes. Add noodles and sauce, stirring constantly until heated through. Add bean sprouts and mix well. Season to taste with freshly ground pepper and serve immediately.

FROM
New World Noodles
by Bill Jones and Stephen Wong

Serves 6 to 8

TIP

The flavor of the chili hinges on the quality of chili powder used. Most powders are a blend of dried, ground mild chilies, as well as cumin, oregano, garlic and salt. Read the list of ingredients to be sure you're not buying one with starch and sugar fillers. Chili powder should not be confused with powdered or ground chilies of the cayenne pepper variety.

FROM
The Comfort Food Cookbook
by Johanna Burkhard

Amazing Chili

1 1/2 lbs	lean ground beef	750 g
2	medium onions, chopped	2
3	cloves garlic, finely chopped	3
2	stalks celery, chopped	2
1	large green bell pepper, chopped	1
2 tbsp	chili powder	25 mL
1 1/2 tsp	dried oregano	7 mL
1 1/2 tsp	ground cumin	7 mL
1 tsp	salt	5 mL
1/2 tsp	red pepper flakes, or to taste	2 mL
1	can (28 oz [796 mL]) tomatoes, chopped, juice reserved	1
1 cup	beef stock	250 mL
1	can (19 oz [540 mL]) pinto *or* red kidney beans, drained and rinsed	1
1/4 cup	chopped fresh parsley *or* coriander	50 mL

1. In a Dutch oven, brown beef over medium-high heat, breaking up with the back of a spoon, for about 7 minutes or until no longer pink.

2. Reduce heat to medium. Add onions, garlic, celery, green pepper, chili powder, oregano, cumin, salt and red pepper flakes; cook, stirring often, for 5 minutes or until vegetables are softened.

3. Stir in the tomatoes with juice and the stock. Bring to a boil; reduce heat, cover and simmer, stirring occasionally, for 1 hour.

4. Add beans and parsley; cover and simmer for 10 minutes more.

Serves 6

Flank Steak in Hoisin Marinade with Sautéed Mushrooms

PREHEAT BROILER OR START BARBECUE

1/4 cup	soya sauce	50 mL
1/4 cup	hoisin sauce	50 mL
1/4 cup	rice wine vinegar	50 mL
2 tbsp	brown sugar	25 mL
2 tbsp	vegetable oil	25 mL
1 tsp	minced ginger root	5 mL
1 tsp	minced garlic	5 mL
1 1/2 lbs	flank steak	750 g
1 tsp	vegetable oil	5 mL
1 tsp	minced garlic	5 mL
3 cups	sliced mushrooms	750 mL
3/4 cup	chopped green onions	175 mL

1. In a small bowl, whisk together soya sauce, hoisin sauce, vinegar, brown sugar, oil, ginger and garlic. Pour over steak and let marinate in the refrigerator for at least 2 hours or overnight. Bring to room temperature before cooking.

2. In a large nonstick skillet, heat oil over medium–high heat. Add garlic and mushrooms and cook for 3 minutes or until softened. Add green onions and cook for 1 minute longer.

3. Barbecue or broil steak, basting with some of the marinade, until cooked to desired "doneness" (approximately 15 minutes). Bring remaining marinade to a boil and simmer for 3 minutes. Serve steak with mushrooms and sauce. Cut the steak across the grain thinly to ensure tenderness.

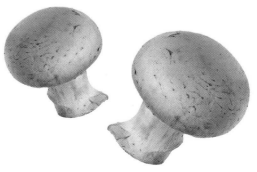

FROM
Rose Reisman's Enlightened
Home Cooking

Pork

Zesty Barbecued Spareribs

Serves 4

TIP

Ribs are great on the barbecue, too. Partially cook ribs in the oven for 45 minutes as directed in the recipe. Complete cooking on a grill over medium-low flame, basting often with the sauce.

Tabasco is the most familiar brand of hot sauce, so we've used it here. But supermarket shelves now boast a large assortment of hot sauces — some quite mild, others having a fiery kick — so experiment with various sauces available and add according to taste

PREHEAT OVEN TO 375° F (190° C)
SHALLOW ROASTING PAN OR BROILER PAN, WITH RACK

3 to 4 lbs	pork spareribs	1.5 to 2 kg
	Salt and pepper	
1 cup	prepared chili sauce *or* ketchup	250 mL
1/2 cup	honey	125 mL
1	small onion, finely chopped	1
2	cloves garlic, minced	2
2 tbsp	Worcestershire sauce	25 mL
2 tbsp	lemon juice	25 mL
1 tbsp	Dijon mustard	15 mL
1 tsp	Tabasco or other hot pepper sauce, or to taste	5 mL
1	lemon, cut into wedges	1

1. Place the ribs on a rack in the roasting pan; season with salt and pepper. Cover with foil. Roast in preheated oven for 45 minutes.

2. In a small saucepan, combine chili sauce, honey, onion, garlic, Worcestershire sauce, lemon juice, mustard and Tabasco sauce. Bring to a boil; reduce heat and simmer, stirring occasionally, for 10 to 15 minutes or until slightly thickened.

3. Remove foil; brush ribs generously on both sides with the sauce. Roast, uncovered, for 45 minutes, brushing generously every 15 minutes with the sauce, until spareribs are nicely glazed and tender.

4. Cut into serving portions; serve with any remaining sauce and lemon wedges.

FROM
The Comfort Food Cookbook
by Johanna Burkhard

Serves 8

TIP

It may appear that you have too much stuffing when you first tie the pork. But once all the strings are in place, it's easy to enclose the meat completely around the fruit mixture.

Company Pork Roast with Fruit Stuffing

PREHEAT OVEN TO 350° F (180° C)
ROASTING PAN WITH RACK

1 tbsp	butter	15 mL
1/3 cup	chopped green onions	75 mL
1 tsp	ground cumin	5 mL
1/2 tsp	curry powder	2 mL
1 cup	chopped mixed dried fruits, such as apricots, prunes, apples, cranberries	250 mL
1/2 cup	soft bread crumbs	125 mL
1 tsp	grated orange rind	5 mL
1	egg, beaten	1
	Salt and pepper	
3 lbs	boneless pork loin roast	1.5 kg
2 tsp	vegetable oil	10 mL
1	large clove garlic, minced	1
1 tsp	rubbed sage	5 mL
1/2 tsp	dried thyme	2 mL
1 tbsp	all-purpose flour	15 mL
1/2 cup	white wine *or* chicken stock	125 mL
3/4 cup	chicken stock	175 mL

1. In a small skillet, melt butter over medium heat. Add green onions, cumin and curry powder; cook, stirring, for 2 minutes or until softened.

2. In a bowl combine onion mixture, dried fruits, bread crumbs, orange rind and egg; season with salt and pepper.

3. Remove the strings from the pork roast; unfold the roast and trim off excess fat. Place pork roast, boned side up, on a work surface. Cover with plastic wrap and pound using a meat mallet to flatten slightly. Season with salt and pepper; spread the stuffing down the center of the meat. Roll the pork around the stuffing and tie securely at 6 intervals with butcher's string.

FROM
The Comfort Food Cookbook
by Johanna Burkhard

4. Place roast on a rack in the roasting pan. In a small bowl, combine oil, garlic, sage and thyme; spread over pork roast and season with salt and pepper.

5. Roast in preheated oven for 1 1/2 to 1 3/4 hours or until the meat thermometer registers 160° F (70° C).

6. Place roast on a cutting board; tent with foil and let stand for 10 minutes before carving.

7. Pour off fat into a pan. Place over medium heat and sprinkle with flour. Cook, stirring, for 1 minute or until lightly colored. Add wine, if using and cook until partially reduced. Add stock and bring to a boil, scraping any brown bits from the bottom of the pan. Season with salt and pepper to taste. Strain sauce through a fine sieve into a warm sauceboat. Cut pork into thick slices and serve accompanied with gravy.

Serves 6

Here's a dish that will be the star of a late-summer *al fresco* supper. Use your barbecue or grill to cook the sausages.

Sausages with Grapes

PREHEAT GRILL OR START BARBECUE

2 lbs	hot Italian sausage (lean, high quality)	1 kg
1 lb	seedless green grapes	500 g
1 lb	seedless red grapes	500 g
2 tbsp	olive oil	25 mL

1. Grill sausages over medium–high heat until cooked through. In a skillet, heat olive oil. Add grapes and toss over medium heat until plumped and heated through, for about 2 minutes. (Alternatively, pan-fry sausages in a little olive oil; remove after 15 minutes or when cooked, add grapes to pan and follow instructions above.)

FROM
Rustic Italian Cooking
by Kathleen Sloan

Serves 4 to 6

For a spicy dipping sauce, combine 2 tsp (10 mL) finely chopped hot chilies, 1 tbsp (15 mL) soya or fish sauce and 1 tsp (5 mL) lime or lemon juice.

Manila Pork Barbecue

1 1/2 lbs	shoulder pork butt, cut into 1-inch (2.5 cm) cubes	750 g
1/2 cup	puréed canned tomatoes *or* puréed, peeled, seeded, fresh tomatoes	125 mL
2 tbsp	soya sauce *or* fish sauce	25 mL
1 tbsp	rice vinegar	15 mL
1 tbsp	minced garlic	15 mL
1 tbsp	finely chopped coriander	15 mL
2 tsp	minced ginger root	10 mL
1 tsp	black pepper	5 mL
6	cloves	6
2	bay leaves, each broken into 2 to 3 pieces	2
1/2 tsp	cayenne pepper *or* finely chopped chilies (optional)	2 mL
4 tsp	granulated sugar	20 mL
4 tsp	olive oil *or* vegetable oil	20 mL
2 tsp	lime or lemon juice	10 mL
	Lime or lemon wedges for garnish	

1. In a shallow glass dish, combine pork, puréed tomatoes, soya sauce, vinegar, garlic, coriander, ginger, pepper, cloves, bay leaves, cayenne (if using) and 2 tsp (10 mL) of the sugar. Cover; marinate at room temperature for 2 hours or overnight in the refrigerator (bring to room temperature before cooking).

2. Drain the meat, reserving marinade and combine with 2 tsp (10 mL) of the oil; thread onto skewers and set aside. In a small saucepan, combine reserved marinade, remaining oil and any juices draining from the skewered meat. Bring to a boil; reduce heat to medium and cook, stirring, for 5 to 8 minutes or until the mixture is fairly dry. Stir in lime juice and remaining sugar; cook for 1 minute longer.

3. Grill skewers over charcoal or under a broiler until cooked through, glazing with the cooked marinade during the last minute of cooking.

FROM
The Asian Bistro Cookbook
by Andrew Chase

Pork Tenderloin Roast with Dried Fruit

PREHEAT OVEN TO 375° F (190° C)

1 1/2 lbs	pork tenderloin	750 g
1/4 cup	brown sugar	50 mL
1/4 cup	orange marmalade	50 mL
1/4 cup	beef stock	50 mL
1/4 cup	red wine	50 mL
1/4 cup	chopped dates	50 mL
1/4 cup	chopped dried apricots	50 mL
1/4 cup	raisins	50 mL

1. Place meat in roasting pan. In a small saucepan, heat sugar and marmalade; brush over pork.

2. Add stock, wine, dates, apricots and raisins to roasting pan.

3. Bake, covered, for 35 to 45 minutes or until no longer pink and the meat thermometer registers 160° to 170° F (70° to 75° C), basting every 10 minutes with pan juices.

4. To serve, slice meat thinly and spoon sauce and fruit over meat.

FROM
Rose Reisman Brings Home
Light Cooking

Serves 4

The trick to this dish is having the noodles ready just as the chops finish cooking. A simple green salad or some pickled vegetables is all you need for a great meal.

FROM
New World Noodles
by Bill Jones and Stephen Wong

Lemon Grass Pork Chops with Chinese Pesto Noodles

1 tbsp	minced garlic	15 mL
1 tbsp	minced ginger root	15 mL
1 tbsp	brown sugar	15 mL
1/4 tsp	5-spice powder	1 mL
1 tbsp	sherry, optional	15 mL
1	lemon grass stalk, smashed and chopped, *or* 2 tsp (10 mL) lemon zest	1
4	6 oz (150 g) pork chops	4
1 tsp	sesame oil	5 mL
1	small chili, seeded and finely chopped	1
1 tbsp	honey	15 mL
8 oz	broad vermicelli (broad rice stick noodles) *or* fettuccine	250 g
1 cup	CHINESE PESTO (recipe follows)	250 mL

1. In a small bowl, combine garlic, ginger, brown sugar, 5-spice powder, sherry and lemon grass. Place pork chops in a dish and spread marinade evenly over them. Cover and marinate, refrigerated, for 4 hours or overnight. Remove from refrigerator 30 minutes before cooking.

2. Preheat broiler or, if using, start barbecue. In a small bowl, combine sesame oil, chili and honey. Set aside.

3. Broil or grill one side of each pork chop until golden brown, for about 6 minutes. Baste the cooked side with sesame oil mixture and continue cooking for 1 minute. Flip chops over and repeat the cooking/basting procedure. The chops should be slightly charred but not burnt.

Recipe continues, next page ...

4. Just before the chops are ready, cook noodles in a large pot of boiling water for 2 minutes. Remove from heat and let soak for 5 minutes. (If using pasta, prepare according to package directions.) Drain, transfer to large bowl, add CHINESE PESTO and toss to mix well.

5. Divide noodles into serving portions. Top each with a pork chop and serve immediately.

Yields 1 cup (250 mL)

A West Coast/Asian variation of the classic Italian pesto. For a treat, try it on grilled oysters.

Chinese Pesto

2 tsp	minced garlic	10 mL
1 cup	toasted hazelnuts	250 mL
1/2 cup	cilantro leaves, well packed	125 mL
2 tbsp	olive oil	25 mL
	Salt and pepper to taste	

1. In a food processor, combine the first 4 ingredients. Process until the mixture becomes a fine paste, scraping down the sides of the bowl once. Season with salt and pepper; pulse until well combined.

FROM
New World Noodles
by Bill Jones and Stephen Wong

Pork Fajitas with Sweet Peppers, Coriander and Cheese

PREHEAT OVEN TO 425° F (220° C)
BAKING SHEET SPRAYED WITH VEGETABLE SPRAY

8 oz	pork tenderloin, cut into thin strips	250 g
2 tsp	vegetable oil	10 mL
1 1/2 tsp	minced garlic	7 mL
1 1/2 cups	thinly sliced onions	375 mL
1 1/2 cups	red pepper strips	375 mL
1/4 cup	fresh chopped coriander *or* parsley	50 mL
3 tbsp	chopped green onions (about 2 medium)	45 mL
6	small flour tortillas	6
1/2 cup	grated Cheddar cheese	125 mL
1/3 cup	bottled salsa	75 mL
1/4 cup	light sour cream	50 mL

1. In a nonstick skillet sprayed with vegetable spray, cook the pork strips over high heat for 2 minutes, or until just done in the center. Remove from the skillet. Add oil. Cook garlic and onions for 4 minutes until browned. Add red pepper strips and cook over medium heat for 5 minutes, or until softened.

2. Remove from heat and stir in coriander, green onions and pork. Divide among the tortillas. Top with cheese, salsa and sour cream. Roll up, place on baking sheet and bake for 5 minutes or until heated through.

FROM
Rose Reisman's
Enlightened Home Cooking

Peppers Stuffed with Capellini and Prosciutto

Serves 6

TIP

Remove pepper skins under cool running water.

Use ham if prosciutto is unavailable.

You can omit the peppers and serve the pasta on its own, sprinkled with grated Parmesan or Romano cheese.

PREHEAT BROILER

6	red or yellow bell peppers	6
12 oz	capellini	375 g
1 tbsp	olive oil	15 mL
1 tsp	minced garlic	5 mL
1 1/4 cups	chicken stock	300 mL
1	large tomato, chopped	1
1/4 cup	butter	50 mL
1 tbsp	chopped fresh basil (or 1 tsp [5 mL] dried)	15 mL
4	slices prosciutto, cut into strips	4
	Pepper to taste	

1. Broil peppers in preheated oven, turning often, for 15 minutes or until charred. Remove from oven and set aside to cool. Then, with a sharp knife, slice off the tops of the peppers and set aside; peel the skin and remove seeds, leaving whole pepper intact.

2. In a large pot of boiling salted water, cook capellini 6 to 8 minutes or until *al dente*. Meanwhile, prepare the sauce.

3. In a large skillet, heat oil over medium-high heat. Add garlic and cook until golden. Stir in chicken stock and tomato; cook for 3 minutes. Reduce heat to medium-low. Stir in butter and basil; mix well.

4. Toss drained pasta with sauce and prosciutto. Season to taste with pepper. Stuff peppers; replace the pepper tops and serve.

FROM
The Robert Rose Book of Classic Pasta

Pork tenderloin is a lean and flavorful meat that can be rapidly cooked to moist perfection.

Since plum sauce has a high sugar content, it will tend to burn; be prepared to lower the heat if the meat starts to brown too quickly.

You can cook the spinach in the same pan as the meat — just add some steamed rice for a complete meal.

FROM
New World Chinese Cooking
by Bill Jones and Stephen Wong

Plum and Chili Glazed Pork Tenderloin

1 lb	pork tenderloin, cut into 1/2-inch (1 cm) slices	500 g
1 tbsp	olive oil	15 mL
1 tbsp	TOASTED CHILI OIL (recipe follows)	15 mL
1 tsp	chili sauce	5 mL
2 tbsp	plum sauce	25 mL
	Salt and pepper to taste	

1. In a bowl combine pork, olive oil, chili oil, chili sauce and plum sauce. Mix well and set aside for 5 minutes.

2. Heat a nonstick skillet over medium-high heat for 30 seconds. Add pork and cook until the bottom is seared and starting to brown, about 4 minutes per side. Reduce heat if the mixture browns too quickly. When pork is cooked through, remove from heat and serve over a vegetable of your choice.

Toasted Chili Oil

2 tbsp	dried chili flakes	25 mL
2 cups	vegetable oil	500 mL

1. In a heavy skillet or small saucepan, heat chili flakes until toasted and almost smoking. Carefully pour in the oil and heat for 1 minute. Remove from heat and allow the flavors to infuse for at least 20 minutes.

2. Transfer to a sterilized glass jar or bottle and refrigerate.

Serves 6

TIP

Black bean sauce is now readily available in the Chinese food section of the grocery store. Ground pork can be replaced with ground beef, veal or chicken.

MAKE AHEAD

Prepare sauce up to a day ahead, stirring before use.

Spaghettini with Minced Pork and Mushrooms in Black Bean Sauce

12 oz	spaghettini	375 g

Sauce

1 1/2 cups	chicken stock	375 mL
1/4 cup	black bean sauce	50 mL
4 tsp	rice wine vinegar	20 mL
4 tsp	soya sauce	20 mL
4 tsp	sesame oil	20 mL
1 tbsp	cornstarch	15 mL
1 tsp	crushed ginger root	5 mL
3 tbsp	brown sugar	45 mL
2 tsp	crushed garlic	10 mL
12 oz	ground pork	375 g
2 tsp	vegetable oil	10 mL
2 cups	sliced mushrooms	500 mL
1 cup	chopped red bell peppers	250 mL
1 tbsp	sesame seeds	15 mL
1/2 cup	chopped green onions	125 mL

1. Cook the pasta in boiling water according to package instructions or until firm to the bite. Drain and place in a serving bowl.

2. Make the sauce: In a small bowl, combine stock, black bean sauce, rice wine vinegar, soya sauce, sesame oil, cornstarch, ginger and sugar; mix well. Set aside.

3. In a large nonstick skillet sprayed with vegetable spray, sauté garlic and pork just until cooked, for approximately 5 minutes. Add oil and sauté mushrooms, red peppers and sesame seeds until vegetables are tender, for approximately 3 minutes.

4. Add the sauce to pork mixture and simmer on low heat until slightly thickened, for approximately 3 minutes, stirring constantly. Pour over pasta. Sprinkle with green onions, and toss.

FROM
Rose Reisman Brings Home Light Pasta

Serves 6 to 8

Radiatore with Sweet Sausage, Zucchini and Tomatoes

TIP

This dish can be made spicier by using spicy sausages and adding 1/4 tsp (1 mL) cayenne pepper.

Beef can be replaced with ground chicken, veal or pork.

MAKE AHEAD

Prepare sauce up to a day ahead, reheating gently before use.

Add some water or beef stock if the sauce thickens.

12 oz	radiatore *or* penne	350 g
2 tsp	vegetable oil	10 mL
2 tsp	crushed garlic	10 mL
3/4 cup	chopped onions	175 mL
3/4 cup	chopped green bell peppers	175 mL
2 cups	chopped zucchini	500 mL
6 oz	sweet sausages, skinned and chopped	150 g
6 oz	ground beef	150 g
2 1/2 cups	canned or fresh tomatoes, crushed	625 mL
1/3 cup	sliced black olives	75 mL
2 tsp	dried basil	10 mL
1 tsp	dried oregano	5 mL

1. Cook pasta in boiling water according to the package instructions or until firm to the bite. Drain and place in a serving bowl.

2. In a large nonstick skillet, heat oil; sauté garlic, onions, green peppers and zucchini until tender, for approximately 5 minutes. Add sausage and beef; sauté just until cooked, approximately 10 minutes. Add tomatoes, olives, basil and oregano; simmer for 15 minutes, until sauce thickens, stirring occasionally. Pour over pasta, and toss.

FROM
Rose Reisman Brings Home Light Pasta

Serves 4

TIP

Inexpensive pork butt or shoulder is the best cut for the stew, but leaner leg meat (fresh ham) can be used.

Use a mild, light-colored vinegar; if you are able to purchase native Filipino palm or nippa sap vinegar, use it here. Serve with rice.

Fresh turmeric root is often available at Southeast Asian or Indian grocers. It has a very raw taste and is best dry-roasted before using. To use here, first toast 1 1/4 tsp (6 mL) very thin slices of turmeric in a dry pan over medium heat until color darkens and the slices become fairly dry; it should be extremely fragrant by then. Either first pound into a powder or add slices directly to the stew.

FROM
The Asian Bistro Cookbook
by Andrew Chase

Filipino Turmeric-Scented Pork Stew

1 1/2 lbs	pork, butt or shoulder, cut into 1 1/2-inch (4 cm) cubes	750 g
1 tsp	minced ginger root	5 mL
1 tbsp	minced garlic	15 mL
3	bay leaves	3
6	cloves *or* 1/4 tsp (1 mL) ground cloves	6
2	2-inch (5 cm) pieces Asian cinnamon stick *or* cinnamon stick	2
1 tsp	ground turmeric	5 mL
1/8 tsp	black pepper	0.5 mL
1/4 cup	rice vinegar	50 mL
3 tbsp	fish sauce *or* 6 finely chopped anchovies mixed in 2 tbsp (25 mL) water	45 mL
1/2 cup	small whole shallots *or* pearl onions (optional)	125 mL
1–1 1/2 cups	peeled, cored and cubed chayote squash *or* green papaya *or* another green-fleshed squash	250–375 mL
1 cup	green peas, fresh or frozen	250 mL
1 3/4 tsp	cornstarch dissolved in 2 tsp (10 mL) water	9 mL
1 tbsp	finely chopped Chinese celery *or* regular celery	15 mL
1 tsp	finely chopped mint *or* parsley (optional)	5 mL

1. In a saucepan combine pork, ginger, garlic, bay leaves, cloves, cinnamon, turmeric, pepper, rice vinegar, fish sauce and shallots, if using; mix well. Let stand 10 to 15 minutes.

2. Bring to a boil, reduce heat to simmer; cover and cook for 45 minutes or until meat is tender. Stir in squash and fresh peas, if using; cook, covered, for 10 minutes or until squash is tender. Stir in frozen peas, if using; cook 1 minute longer. Bring to a boil and stir in cornstarch mixture; reduce heat to simmer and cook 1 minute. Stir in celery; cook for 20 seconds. Serve garnished with mint or parsley, if desired.

Serves 6

Years ago I lived in a tiny bedsitter in the north London district of Muswell Hill, where I recall subsisting mostly on risotto, Leicester cheese, Branston pickle and Jacob's Cream Crackers. But once a week, the young Welsh newlywed who lived down the hall would make her husband's favorite — "spag bol," as they short-form it in England — and occasionally she would invite me in for a taste. At the time I thought it delicious, due in large part, no doubt, to my growling tum.

Many years later in Italy I tasted the real thing and learned that, in fact, the Bolognese would never dream of eating this meaty sauce with spaghetti — preferring tagliatelle, maccheroni, fettuccine or rigatoni. I like it best with long-cut ziti, but would enjoy it just as much simply spooned onto good bread! Use this sauce to make the world's greatest lasagna.

Although some versions of this dish call for the addition of tomatoes, I prefer to use a small amount of good tomato paste.

FROM
Rustic Italian Cooking
by Kathleen Sloan

Ragù Bolognese
(Bolognese Sauce)

1/4 cup	olive oil	50 mL
2	cloves garlic, finely chopped	2
1	onion, finely diced	1
1	carrot, finely diced	1
2	stalks celery, finely diced	2
12 oz	extra lean ground beef	375 g
12 oz	pork loin, finely chopped *or* lean ground pork	375 g
4 oz	pancetta, finely chopped	125 g
3	plump fresh chicken livers, washed, trimmed and finely chopped	3
Pinch	freshly grated nutmeg	Pinch
1 cup	red wine	250 mL
1 tbsp	tomato paste	15 mL
1/2 tsp	salt	2 mL
1/4 tsp	freshly ground black pepper	1 mL
1 tsp	coarse salt	5 mL
1 lb	tagliatelle *or* maccheroni *or* fettuccine	500 g
1 cup	grated Parmigiano-Reggiano	250 mL

1. In a large skillet, heat olive oil over medium heat. Add garlic and onion; cook for 3 minutes or until softened. Stir in carrot and celery; cook, stirring occasionally, for 10 minutes or until vegetables are softened.

2. Add beef, pork, pancetta, chicken livers and nutmeg; cook, stirring to break up meat, for 10 minutes or until meat is browned. Stir in red wine. Bring to a boil; cook for 5 minutes. Stir together tomato paste and 1/2 cup (125 mL) warm water; stir into meat mixture. Return to a boil, reduce heat to low and stir in salt and pepper. Cover and cook for 1 1/2 to 2 hours, stirring occasionally, or until meat is very tender. If ragù appears too dry as it cooks, add a little more water or wine

3. When ragù is almost finished, bring a large pot of water to a boil. Stir in coarse salt. Cook pasta until tender but firm; drain and transfer to a warmed serving bowl. Pour ragù over pasta; toss to coat. Serve immediately, sprinkled with Parmigiano-Reggiano.

Crispy-skinned and succulent roasted pork, sold by the pound, is one of our favorite treats from the Chinese barbecue shop. It's hard not to eat it right away, but if there's anything left, this is a great way to use it up.

Braised Roasted Pork with Tofu and Green Onions

4	dried Chinese black mushrooms	4
1 tbsp	vegetable oil	15 mL
5	thin slices ginger root	5
1 tsp	minced garlic	5 mL
1 lb	Crispy-skin roasted pork *or* barbecued pork *or* leftover roast pork, cut into 1/2-inch (1 cm) slices	500 g
2 tbsp	oyster sauce	25 mL
1 tbsp	soya sauce	15 mL
1 tbsp	dark soya sauce	15 mL
1/2 cup	chicken stock or water	125 mL
	Salt and freshly ground black pepper to taste	
1 tbsp	cornstarch, dissolved in 2 tbsp (25 mL) chicken stock *or* water	15 mL
2	packages (10 oz [300 g]) soft tofu, cut into pieces 1 inch (2.5 cm) by 1/2 inch (1 cm)	2
3	green onions, cut into 1-inch (2.5 cm) lengths	3

1. In a heatproof bowl, soak the mushrooms in boiling water for 15 minutes. Remove the stems, slice the caps thinly and set aside.

2. In a wok or deep skillet, heat oil over medium–high heat. Add ginger root, garlic and mushrooms and sauté until fragrant (for about 1 minute). Add pork and stir-fry for 1 minute. Add oyster sauce, soya sauces and stock; mix well, reduce heat to medium and cook for 3 minutes. Season to taste with salt and pepper. Add the dissolved cornstarch and cook until the sauce is thickened.

3. Gently fold tofu and green onions into the mixture; cover and allow to absorb flavors for 2 minutes. Transfer to a deep platter and serve immediately.

FROM
New World Chinese Cooking
by Bill Jones and Stephen Wong

Serves 4 to 6

This is a slightly fancier version of a traditional home-style Thai dish that is full-flavored (but not spicy), peppery and sweet. At the restaurant, I prepared this stew with quail eggs, which are readily available at Chinese poultry stores and grocers, but harder to find elsewhere. The single-bite size and fine taste of quail eggs make the presentation quite nice, but chicken eggs are good, too. Choose smaller eggs, such as the economical "pee-wee" size.

Chances are you won't be able to find fresh bamboo shoots — and even if you do, they'll be extremely pricey. So use the canned variety: either Chinese winter bamboo shoots or whole bamboo shoots imported from Thailand or China. Sliced bamboo shoots (which seem to be more available in regular supermarkets) are not ideally suited to this dish, but can be used in a pinch.

FROM
The Asian Bistro Cookbook
by Andrew Chase

Thai Sweet Pork Stew with Eggs

6	cloves garlic	6
4	stalks coriander, with roots	4
4	green onions	4
1	chopped green finger chili *or* 4 green bird-eye chilies	1
2 tsp	chopped ginger root	10 mL
1 tbsp	coriander seeds *or* 2 tsp (10 mL) ground coriander	15 mL
2 1/2 tsp	black peppercorns *or* 1 1/2 tsp (7 mL) ground black pepper	12 mL
1/2 tsp	cumin seeds *or* 1/4 tsp (1 mL) ground cumin	2 mL
6	cloves *or* 1/4 tsp (1 mL) ground cloves	6
6	small chicken eggs *or* 12 quail eggs	6
1 tbsp	vegetable oil	15 mL
1 1/2 lbs	pork shoulder or butt, preferably with skin attached, cut into 1-inch (2.5 cm) cubes	750 g
1	can (10 oz [284 mL]) unsliced or winter bamboo shoots (from China or Thailand), rinsed and drained, cut into 1-inch (2.5 cm) cubes	1
1/2 cup	fish sauce *or* 9 anchovies, chopped	125 mL
1/3 cup	sugar (preferably palm sugar)	75 mL
1 1/2 tsp	cornstarch dissolved in 1 tbsp (15 mL) water (optional)	7 mL
24	mint leaves, chopped	24

As in most Thai dishes, palm sugar is the preferred sweetener. This type of sugar is used widely throughout Southeast Asia, including the Philippines, and India (where it is called "jaggery") and can be purchased at many ethnic grocery stores. It is a light- to medium-brown color and is usually sold in small cakes in various sizes and shapes, depending on the country of origin. Palm sugar is easily grated or crumbled and has its own flavor, much as maple sugar does. It's worth picking some up if you see it at the store. It will keep indefinitely, although it sometimes melts a little and gets sticky in warm weather; but this does not affect the flavor. I find the best substitute to be a half-and-half mixture of white and brown sugar. Chinese pressed block sugar or yellow rock sugar are also good products.

1. In a food processor, combine garlic, coriander, green onions, chilies and ginger; chop as finely as possible. Set aside. In a dry frying pan over medium heat, toast in separate batches the coriander seeds, peppercorns, cumin seeds and cloves until fragrant; or, combine ground spices and toast. Set aside. In a saucepan add cold water to cover the eggs; bring to a boil, remove from heat, cover and let stand for 5 minutes for chicken eggs or 3 minutes for quail eggs. Cool in cold water; peel and set aside.

2. In a heavy-bottomed saucepan, heat the oil over medium-high heat; brown the pork in 2 batches. Return all pork to the saucepan. Stir in green paste; cook, stirring constantly, for 3 minutes. Stir in dry spices and bamboo shoots; cook, stirring, 1 minute. Stir in fish sauce, sugar and 3/4 cup (175 mL) water; bring to a boil, reduce heat to simmer, cover and cook for 20 minutes. Add eggs to stew. If necessary, add additional water just to cover the meat.

3. Cook, covered, for 40 minutes longer or until pork is tender. Uncover, bring to a boil and cook until the sauce thickens slightly. If the pork was cooked with the skin, the sauce should be thick enough to coat a spoon; if the pork was skinless or if you want a thicker sauce, stir in cornstarch mixture and cook for 1 minute longer.

4. Halve the chicken eggs, if using. Serve stew garnished with mint. Serve with white rice.

Crispy wisps of oven-roasted chow mein enhance any meal, especially with an accent of garlic and fresh herbs. If you're using dry herbs use only the suggested amounts — their flavor is very concentrated.

Oven-Roasted Chow Mein with Mixed Herbs, Olive Oil and Garlic

PREHEAT OVEN TO 350° F (180° C)
OVENPROOF SKILLET OR 13- BY 9-INCH (3 L) BAKING DISH

1 lb	fresh chow mein noodles	500 g
2 tbsp	olive oil, plus oil for coating noodles	25 mL
1 tbsp	minced garlic	15 mL
1 tbsp	finely chopped fresh basil (or 1/2 tsp [2 mL] dried)	15 mL
1 tsp	finely chopped rosemary (fresh or dried)	5 mL
1 tsp	finely chopped sage (or pinch dried)	5 mL
	Salt and pepper	

1. In a heatproof bowl or pot, cover the noodles with boiling water and soak for 5 minutes. Drain and toss with a little oil.

2. In an ovenproof skillet, heat oil for 30 seconds. Add noodles and stir-fry until well coated. Sprinkle with garlic and herbs. Season with salt and pepper; mix well.

3. Place the skillet in the oven (or transfer to a baking dish, if using) and roast for 15 minutes or until the noodles are crisp and golden. Serve immediately.

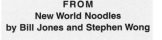

FROM
New World Noodles
by Bill Jones and Stephen Wong

Hazelnut Pork Chops

Serves 2

TIP

Hazelnut flour is available in many grocery stores; but if you can't find any, just buy raw hazelnuts and grind them fine in a blender or coffee grinder.

Frangelico (hazelnut liqueur) is ideal here, but if you don't want to fork out for a whole bottle, use whatever booze you have on hand — rum, brandy or any liqueur.

1 tsp	butter	5 mL
1	pear, cored, peeled and cut into 1/2-inch (1 cm) slices	1
1 tbsp	water	15 mL
1 tsp	whole-grain mustard	5 mL
1	egg	1
1/4 cup	milk	50 mL
1/4 cup	vegetable oil	50 mL
4	pork chops, 1/2 inch (1 cm) thick, about 12 oz (375 g)	4 in all
1/2 cup	all-purpose flour	125 mL
1/2 cup	hazelnut flour *or* finely ground hazelnuts	125 mL
2 tbsp	Frangelico *or* other hazelnut liqueur	25 mL
	Salt and pepper	
	Few sprigs fresh parsley, chopped	

1. In a small nonstick frying pan, melt butter over medium heat. Add pears and sauté, gently turning, for 2 to 3 minutes or until soft and starting to brown. Add water and mustard; gently toss for 1 minute until well mixed. Remove from heat; reserve in frying pan.

2. In a small bowl, beat egg with milk; set aside. In a large frying pan, heat oil over medium-high heat for 1 minute or until quite hot. Meanwhile, quickly dredge the pork chops in the all-purpose flour and dunk them in the egg-milk mixture; dredge both sides in hazelnut flour. Carefully add to hot oil, reduce heat to medium and cook each side for 2 to 3 minutes or until golden brown and cooked through. Drain on paper towels.

3. Return pears to high heat; cook for 1 minute or until sizzling. Add Frangelico; cook, shaking the pan, for 1 to 2 minutes or until sizzling and evaporating.

4. Immediately portion out the pears onto 2 plates. Place 2 pork chops on top of the pears on each plate. Season with salt and pepper and garnish with parsley. Serve immediately.

FROM
Simply Mediterranean Cooking
by Byron Ayanoglu and
Algis Kemezys

**Serves 4
as a side dish**

TIP

Wild rice can be replaced with brown or white rice or a combination. Cook white rice for only 15 to 20 minutes; allow 35 minutes for brown rice.

For a spicier version of this dish, try adding 1/2 tsp (2 mL) chili powder

MAKE AHEAD

Prepare up to 1 day in advance and bake just before serving.

**FROM
Rose Reisman's Light
Vegetarian Cooking**

Zucchini Stuffed with Rice and Mushrooms

**PREHEAT OVEN TO 350° F (180° C)
13- BY 9-INCH (3 L) BAKING DISH SPRAYED WITH VEGETABLE SPRAY**

3 cups	vegetable stock	750 mL
1/2 cup	wild rice	125 mL
2	large zucchini (each about 8 oz [250 g])	2
1 tsp	vegetable oil	5 mL
2 tsp	minced garlic	10 mL
3/4 cup	chopped onions	175 mL
2 cups	sliced mushrooms	500 mL
1 1/2 tsp	drained capers	7 mL
1 tsp	dried basil	5 mL
1/2 tsp	dried oregano	2 mL
3/4 cup	prepared tomato pasta sauce	175 mL
3 tbsp	grated Parmesan cheese (optional)	45 mL

1. In a small saucepan, bring stock to a boil; stir in rice, cover, reduce heat to low and cook for 35 to 40 minutes or until the rice is tender. Drain any excess liquid.

2.. Meanwhile, cut each zucchini in half lengthwise. In a large pot of boiling water, cook the zucchini for 4 minutes; drain. When cool enough to handle, carefully scoop out the pulp, leaving shells intact. Chop pulp and set aside. Put zucchini shells into prepared baking dish.

3. In a large nonstick frying pan sprayed with vegetable spray, heat oil over medium-high heat. Add garlic and onions; cook for 3 minutes or until softened. Stir in mushrooms, capers, basil and oregano; cook for 5 minutes or until the mushrooms are browned. Stir in zucchini pulp; cook for 2 minutes. Remove from heat.

4. Stir cooked rice, tomato sauce and 1 tbsp (15 mL) of the Parmesan cheese, if desired, into vegetable mixture. Stuff mixture evenly into zucchini boats, mounding filling high. Sprinkle with remaining Parmesan, if desired. Cover dish tightly with foil.

5. Bake 15 minutes or until heated through.

Lamb

Grilled Lamb Chops with Mustard

Serves 2

Lamb is the preferred meat of Mediterranean gods and nothing makes it more divinely succulent than the quick sear of a barbecue.

This recipe uses a full-flavored coating to protect the delicate lamb from the rigors of the grill. While fresh local lamb is obviously the best, even frozen (if slowly defrosted) meat works, since the mustard coating compensates for the loss of flavor.

PREHEAT GRILL OR BROILER

1 tbsp	whole-grain mustard	15 mL
1 tsp	Dijon mustard	5 mL
1 tbsp	olive oil	15 mL
1/2 tsp	dried thyme	2 mL
1/2 tsp	crumbled dried rosemary	2 mL
1/4 tsp	black pepper	1 mL
4	lamb chops, 1 inch (2.5 cm) thick (about 1 1/4 lbs [625 g])	4
	Salt to taste	
1 tbsp	lemon juice	15 mL
	Few sprigs fresh parsley, chopped	
2	green onions, finely chopped	2

1. In a small bowl, stir together the mustards, olive oil, thyme, rosemary and black pepper until smooth. Generously brush both sides of the chops with this mixture and let rest at room temperature for about 30 minutes.

2. Grill or broil lamb chops to your preference (3 to 4 minutes each side for medium rare). Sprinkle salt and lemon juice on the chops. Serve immediately, garnished with chopped parsley and green onions.

FROM
Simply Mediterranean Cooking by
Byron Ayanoglu & Algis Kemezys

Serves 8

Lamb is often my first choice when planning a special dinner. It's always a crowd pleaser. I love the heavenly aroma of garlic and rosemary in this recipe — it fills my house and makes an especially warm welcome for friends as they come through the door. Take the lamb out of the fridge about 30 minutes before roasting. Choose potatoes that are the same size so they roast evenly. As for the white wine, if you don't want to open a bottle, a good substitute is dry white vermouth. Keep a bottle handy in the cupboard for those recipes that call for white wine.

FROM
The Comfort Food Cookbook
by Johanna Burkhard

Rosemary Roast Lamb with New Potatoes

PREHEAT OVEN TO 350° F (180° C)
LARGE, SHALLOW ROASTING PAN, OILED

8	cloves garlic	8
1	leg of lamb, 5 to 6 lbs (2.5 to 3 kg)	1
	Grated rind and juice of 1 lemon	
2 tbsp	olive oil	25 mL
1 tbsp	dried rosemary, crumbled	15 mL
1/2 tsp	salt	2 mL
1/2 tsp	pepper	2 mL
3 lbs	whole new potatoes, scrubbed (about 12)	1.5 kg
1 tbsp	all-purpose flour	15 mL
1/2 cup	white wine	125 mL
1 cup	chicken stock	250 mL

1. Cut 6 cloves garlic into 8 to 10 slivers each. Using the tip of a knife, cut shallow slits all over lamb and insert a garlic sliver into each.

2. Finely chop remaining 2 garlic cloves. In a bowl, combine garlic, lemon juice and rind, oil, rosemary, salt and pepper. Place lamb in prepared roasting pan; surround with potatoes. Brush lamb and potatoes generously with lemon-garlic mixture. Insert meat thermometer into thickest part of leg.

3. Roast in preheated oven for about 1 1/2 hours, turning potatoes over halfway through roasting, until meat thermometer registers 135° F (57° C) for medium-rare. (For medium, remove the potatoes and continue to roast lamb for 15 to 20 minutes more or to your liking.)

4. Remove lamb to a platter; tent with foil and let rest for 10 minutes before carving. Transfer potatoes to a dish; keep warm.

5. Skim the fat in pan; place over medium heat. Stir in flour and cook, stirring, until lightly colored. Pour in wine; cook, scraping up any brown bits until wine is reduced by half. Stir in stock; bring to a boil, stirring, until thickened. Strain through a fine sieve into a warm sauceboat.

6. Carve the lamb. Arrange slices on serving plate and moisten with some of the sauce; surround with roasted potatoes. Serve with remaining sauce.

Asparagus with Parmesan and Toasted Almonds

Serves 6

When locally grown asparagus appears at the market, it's one of my rites of spring. I prepare them tossed with crunchy almonds and melting Parmesan — and it's every bit as pleasing as a buttery Hollandaise.

TIP

Try making this dish with green beans. Trim and cut into 1 1/2-inch (4 cm) lengths and cook in boiling water for about 5 minutes or until tender-crisp.

1 1/2 lbs	asparagus	750 g
1/4 cup	sliced blanched almonds	50 mL
2 tbsp	butter	25 mL
2	cloves garlic, finely chopped	2
1/4 cup	freshly grated Parmesan cheese	50 mL
	Salt and pepper	

1. Snap off asparagus ends. Cut the spears on a diagonal into 2-inch (5 cm) lengths. In a large nonstick skillet, bring 1/2 cup (125 mL) water to a boil; cook the asparagus for 2 minutes (start timing when water returns to a boil) or until just tender-crisp. Run under cold water to chill; drain and reserve.

2. Dry the skillet; heat over medium heat. Add the almonds and toast, stirring often, for 2 to 3 minutes or until golden. Remove and reserve.

3. Increase heat to medium-high. Add butter to skillet; cook asparagus and garlic, stirring, for 4 minutes or until the asparagus is just tender.

4. Sprinkle with Parmesan; season with salt and pepper. Transfer to serving bowl; top with almonds.

FROM
The Comfort Food Cookbook
by Johanna Burkhard

Serves 4

Greek Chili with Black Olives and Feta Cheese

TIP

Leave the skin on zucchini and eggplant for extra fiber.

Other canned beans can be used, such as chick peas, navy white beans or black beans.

Another cheese can replace feta, such as goat, Cheddar or mozzarella.

MAKE AHEAD

Prepare up to a day ahead and gently reheat, adding more stock if too thick.

Great as leftovers.

1 tsp	vegetable oil	5 mL
2 tsp	minced garlic	10 mL
1 cup	chopped onions	250 mL
1 cup	chopped zucchini	250 mL
1 cup	sliced mushrooms	250 mL
1 cup	chopped green peppers	250 mL
1 1/2 cups	chopped eggplant	375 mL
8 oz	lean ground lamb or beef	250 g
1 cup	canned red kidney beans, drained	250 mL
1 cup	canned white kidney beans, drained	250 mL
1	can (19 oz [540 mL]) tomatoes, puréed	1
1 1/2 cups	beef or chicken stock	375 mL
1/3 cup	sliced black olives	75 mL
1 tbsp	chili powder	15 mL
1 1/2 tsp	dried basil	7 mL
1 1/2 tsp	dried oregano	7 mL
2 oz	feta cheese, crumbled	50 g

1. In a large nonstick saucepan sprayed with vegetable spray, heat oil over medium heat. Add garlic, onions, zucchini, mushrooms, green peppers and eggplant; cook for 8 minutes or until softened. Add lamb and cook for 2 minutes, stirring to break it up, or until it is no longer pink. Drain any excess fat.

2. Mash 1/2 cup (125 mL) of the red kidney beans and 1/2 cup (125 mL) of the white kidney beans. Add tomatoes, stock, mashed and whole beans, olives, chili, basil and oregano to saucepan; bring to a boil. Reduce heat to low and simmer, covered, for 30 minutes. Sprinkle with cheese before serving.

FROM
Rose Reisman's Enlightened
Home Cooking

Mint and Coriander Marinated Lamb

Serves 6

Here we marinate lamb (racks or leg) in a fragrant mix of mint, coriander and other herbs and spices, then roast it. The marinade is inspired by Vietnamese and Thai marinades, with a touch of Malay spicing. Lamb brochettes can also be marinated in this style, then grilled (see Variation).

ROASTING PAN WITH RACK

3	racks of lamb (each about 350 g) or 1 leg of lamb (about 3 to 4 lbs [1.5 to 2 kg] bone-in, or 2 to 3 lbs [1 to 1.5 kg] boneless)	3
3/4 cup	roughly chopped coriander, leaves and stems	175 mL
3/4 cup	roughly chopped mint leaves	175 mL
2 tbsp	chopped fresh galangal or 1 1/2 tbsp (20 mL) chopped ginger root	25 mL
2 tbsp	lime juice	25 mL
6	anchovies	6
6	cloves garlic	6
5	seeded and roughly chopped green finger chilies	5
3	shallots	3
3 to 6	green bird-eye chilies (optional)	3 to 6
1 tbsp	fennel seeds	15 mL
10	cloves or 1/2 tsp (2 mL) ground cloves	10
1 1/2 tsp	black peppercorns or 1 tsp (5 mL) ground black pepper	7 mL
1 tsp	cumin seeds or 3/4 tsp (4 mL) ground cumin	5 mL
1 tsp	coriander seeds or 3/4 tsp (4 mL) ground coriander	5 mL
1	2-inch (5-cm) piece cinnamon stick or 3/4 tsp (4 mL) ground cinnamon	1
2 tsp	vegetable oil	10 mL

1. Trim most, but not all, of the surface fat from the racks or leg. Place in a shallow glass baking dish.

2. In a food processor, combine coriander, mint, galangal, lime juice, anchovies, garlic, finger chilies, shallots and bird-eye chilies, if using; purée until finely chopped. Toast fennel seed, cloves, peppercorns, cumin seed,

FROM
The Asian Bistro Cookbook
by Andrew Chase

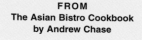

coriander seeds and cinnamon stick separately in a dry frying pan over medium heat until fragrant; or toast the fennel seeds and combine the remaining dry ground spices and toast. Grind the whole spices except the fennel seeds together to a fine powder. Mix ground spices, whole toasted fennel seeds and oil into the marinade paste and spread over the lamb. Cover; marinate for at least 4 hours at room temperature or overnight in the refrigerator (bring to room temperature before cooking).

3. Transfer to roasting pan. Cook in a preheated 325° F (160° C) oven 40 minutes for the racks or 1 1/2 hour for the leg. Let rest 5 minutes; cut the racks into separate ribs pieces or carve the leg into thin slices. Serve with pan juices, if any, and accompany with chutney, if desired.

Variation

Lamb brochettes, cut from the leg, are very good prepared in this marinade. Alternate 2 lbs (1 kg) lamb pieces marinated in the above paste with 18 large white or cremini mushrooms marinated in 2 tsp (10 mL) lime juice, 1 tbsp (15 mL) vegetable oil and 1 tsp (5 mL) fish sauce or 1/4 tsp (1 mL) salt. If desired, pieces of green chilies or pepper can be threaded on the skewers. Grill over medium heat.

Serves 4 to 6

To make stuffing shells easier, carefully cut up one side with a pair of scissors; lay flat, stuff and roll.

Lamb Cannelloni with Walnut Parmesan Sauce

PREHEAT OVEN TO 375° F (190° C)
13- BY 9-INCH (3 L) BAKING DISH

12	cannelloni shells	12
1 tbsp	olive oil	15 mL
8 oz	lamb, cut into cubes	250 g
1 tbsp	chopped fresh rosemary (or 1 tsp [5 mL] dried)	15 mL
1 tsp	minced garlic	5 mL
1/2 cup	chopped onions	125 mL
2 tbsp	chopped fresh parsley (or 1 1/2 tsp [7 mL] dried)	25 mL
1/4 cup	seasoned bread crumbs	50 mL
	Salt and pepper to taste	
1	egg	1
Sauce		
2 tbsp	butter	25 mL
1 cup	whipping (35%) cream	250 mL
2 tbsp	grated Parmesan cheese	25 mL
2 tsp	minced fresh parsley	10 mL
2 tsp	finely chopped toasted walnuts	10 mL

1. In a large pot of boiling salted water, cook cannelloni for 10 to 12 minutes or until tender; drain. Rinse under cold water, drain and set aside.

2. In a large skillet, heat oil over medium–high heat. Add lamb, rosemary, garlic and onions; cook until the lamb is medium done. Stir in parsley. Transfer to a food processor; purée with bread crumbs. Season to taste with salt and pepper. Add egg; process until well-mixed. Stuff shells and place in the baking dish.

3. Make the sauce: In a saucepan, bring butter, cream, Parmesan, parsley and walnuts to a boil; pour over shells. Cover dish tightly with aluminum foil.

4. Bake until hot, for about 15 minutes.

FROM
The Robert Rose Book of
Classic Pasta

Serves 2

Here's another idea for lamb chops on the barbecue.

This Levantine interpretation uses thin chops, charred to exuberantly juicy tenderness on the red-hot coals of small braziers in a white-washed courtyard by the seaside. The flavored yogurt acts both as sauce and condiment; together they'll recall for you warm-weather feasting during jasmine-scented nights.

Grilled Lamb Chops with Minted Yogurt

PREHEAT BROILER

6	lamb chops, 1/4 to 1/2 inch (5 mm to 1 cm) thick, about 1 lb (500 g) in all	6
1 tbsp	olive oil	15 mL
1/2 tsp	dried oregano	2 mL
1/4 tsp	freshly ground black pepper	1 mL
1/2 cup	thinly sliced onions	125 mL
1/2 cup	yogurt	125 mL
1	clove garlic, pressed	1
2 tbsp	chopped fresh mint (or 1/2 tsp [2 mL] dried)	25 mL
1 tbsp	lemon juice	15 mL
1 tsp	extra virgin olive oil	5 mL
	Salt and pepper to taste	
1/2 tsp	dried oregano	2 mL

1. Brush lamb chops with olive oil and lay out on a flat plate. Sprinkle with 1/2 tsp (2 mL) oregano and 1/4 tsp (1 mL) freshly ground black pepper; top with the onions, pressing down into the meat. Cover and let marinate at room temperature for 20 minutes.

2. In a small bowl, combine yogurt, garlic, mint, lemon juice, olive oil, salt and pepper. Mix to integrate well, cover and let rest up to 30 minutes, unrefrigerated. (This sauce can be prepared in advance and refrigerated. It must be allowed a 30-minute "warm-up" to room temperature and a stir before being served.)

3. Grill or broil lamb chops (with any onions that happen to stick on) for 2 to 3 minutes each side or until done to your liking. Sprinkle with dried oregano just before taking off the grill.

4. Spread a thick quantity of the yogurt sauce on each of 2 warmed plates. Transfer 3 chops onto the middle of sauce on each plate and serve immediately.

FROM
Simply Mediterranean Cooking by
Byron Ayanoglu & Algis Kemezys

Serves 4

Roasted Rack of Lamb with Onion Jam

This recipe comes from the talented culinary students and their instructors at the Southern Alberta Institute of Technology.

Make extra onion jam and use it to top savory sandwiches or pizzas, or as an appetizer with French bread.

To "french" lamb racks, remove spine bone and trim all of the meat, fat and sinew away from the ends of the rib bones.

Serves 4

2	racks Alberta lamb (7 ribs each), frenched	2
1 tbsp	olive oil	15 mL

Marinade

1 cup	coarse-grained Dijon mustard	250 mL
1	sprig fresh rosemary, leaves only	1
8	black peppercorns, crushed	8
2	cloves garlic, crushed	2

Onion jam

2 tbsp	butter	25 mL
8 oz	onions *or* shallots, peeled and sliced	250 g
1/4 cup	white wine	50 mL
2 tbsp	granulated sugar	25 mL

Sauce

2 tbsp	red wine	25 mL
2 cups	lamb stock *or* beef stock	500 mL
1	clove garlic, crushed	1
1/2 tsp	chopped fresh rosemary	2 mL
	Salt and pepper to taste	
	Steamed vegetables and roasted potatoes as accompaniments	

1. Marinade: In a food processor, combine mustard, rosemary, peppercorns and garlic; purée until smooth. With a brush, generously coat the entire racks of lamb with the marinade. Cover and refrigerate overnight.

2. Onion jam: In a heavy saucepan, melt butter over medium heat. Stir in onions, sugar and white wine. Reduce heat to medium-low and cook, uncovered and stirring occasionally, 30 minutes or until onions are soft and caramelized. Set aside. (Jam can be made in advance and reheated before serving.)

FROM
The Wild West Cookbook
by Cinda Chavich

Recipe continues, next page …

3. Bring lamb to room temperature. Preheat oven to 375° F (190° C). In an ovenproof frying pan, heat olive oil over medium-high heat. One at a time, cook lamb racks, turning occasionally, for 4 minutes or until well browned. Return both racks to pan; stand them up, interlocking the rib bones. Roast for 30 minutes or until a meat thermometer reads 130° F (65° C) for medium–rare.

4. Remove lamb from pan, tent with foil and keep warm. Discard the fat in the pan and stir the red wine into the pan drippings. Bring to a boil, scraping browned bits off the bottom of the pan. Add the stock, garlic and rosemary. Boil until reduced to about 3/4 cup (175 mL). Strain sauce and season to taste with salt and pepper.

5. Carve the lamb with a sharp knife, cutting between the ribs. Arrange the lamb over a mound of warm onion jam on each of four plates, with rib bones pointing up at the center of the plate. Drizzle with sauce and serve with steamed vegetables and roasted potatoes.

Serves 4 to 6

This simple side dish requires the freshest walnuts — so buy them unshelled if available. To boost the flavor, briefly toast unchopped walnuts in the oven on a baking sheet; keep a careful eye on them, since they can burn quickly.

Endive with Walnuts and Pancetta

6-CUP (1.5 L) GRATIN DISH OR OTHER OVENPROOF DISH

3 tbsp	olive oil	45 mL
4 oz	pancetta, finely chopped	125 g
2	cloves garlic, finely chopped	2
6	Belgian endives, washed, trimmed and cut in half lengthwise	6
1/2 cup	dry white wine	125 mL
1/4 tsp	salt	1 mL
1/4 tsp	freshly ground black pepper	1 mL
1 cup	grated Parmigiano-Reggiano	250 mL
1 cup	walnut halves, chopped (reserve a few, unchopped, for garnish)	250 mL

1. In a large skillet, heat the olive oil over medium heat. Add pancetta and garlic; cook for 3 minutes. Do not let the garlic brown. Add endives; cook for 3 minutes, turning once or twice with tongs. Arrange endives cut-side down. Pour in wine; sprinkle with salt and pepper. Cover skillet, reduce heat to medium-low and cook for 10 minutes or until the endives are tender. Preheat broiler.

2. Transfer the cooked endives and skillet contents to gratin dish. Sprinkle with grated Parmigiano-Reggiano. Broil for 2 minutes or until the cheese is lightly browned. Sprinkle with chopped walnuts. Serve immediately, garnished with halved walnuts.

FROM
Rustic Italian Cooking
by Kathleen Sloan

Curried Lamb Casserole with Sweet Potatoes

12 oz	lamb, cut into 3/4-inch (2 cm) cubes	375 g
	All-purpose flour for dusting	
1 tbsp	vegetable oil	15 mL
2 tsp	crushed garlic	10 mL
1 cup	chopped onion	250 mL
1 cup	finely chopped carrots	250 mL
1/2 cup	finely chopped green bell pepper	125 mL
1 cup	cubed peeled sweet potatoes	250 mL
1 1/2 cups	sliced mushrooms	375 mL
2 1/2 cups	beef stock	625 mL
1/3 cup	red wine	75 mL
3 tbsp	tomato paste	45 mL
2 tsp	curry powder	10 mL

1. Dust lamb with flour.

2. In a large nonstick Dutch oven, heat oil, sauté lamb for 2 minutes or just until seared all over. Remove lamb and set aside.

3. To skillet, add garlic, onion, carrots, green pepper and sweet potatoes; cook, stirring often, for 8 to 10 minutes or until tender. Add mushrooms and cook until softened, for approximately 3 minutes.

4. Add stock, wine, tomato paste and curry powder. Return lamb to pan; cover and simmer for 1 1/2 hours, stirring occasionally.

FROM
Rose Reisman Brings Home
Light Cooking

Lamb Vegetable Stew over Garlic Mashed Potatoes

3 tsp	vegetable oil	15 mL
12 oz	leg of lamb, visible fat removed, cut into 1-inch (2.5 cm) cubes	375 g
3 tbsp	flour	45 mL
1 cup	pearl onions	250 mL
2 tsp	minced garlic	10 mL
1 1/2 cups	sliced mushrooms	375 mL
1 1/2 cups	chopped leeks	375 mL
1 cup	sliced carrots	250 mL
1 cup	chopped green or yellow peppers	250 mL
3/4 cup	sliced zucchini	175 mL
1/4 cup	tomato paste	50 mL
1/3 cup	red or white wine	75 mL
2 cups	chopped tomatoes	500 mL
2 cups	beef or chicken stock	500 mL
2 tsp	dried rosemary	10 mL
1	bay leaf	1

Mashed Potatoes

1 1/2 lbs	potatoes, peeled and quartered	750 g
1 tbsp	margarine *or* butter	15 mL
1 tbsp	minced garlic	15 mL
1 cup	chopped onion	250 mL
1/2 cup	chicken stock	125 mL
1/3 cup	light sour cream	75 mL
1/4 tsp	ground black pepper	1 mL

1. In a large nonstick saucepan, heat 2 tsp (10 mL) of the oil over medium-high heat. Dust the lamb cubes in the flour and add to the saucepan. Cook for 5 minutes or until well-browned on all sides. Remove the lamb from the saucepan.

2. Blanch the pearl onions in a pot of boiling water for 1 minute; refresh in cold water and drain. Peel and set aside.

Recipe continues, next page ...

FROM
Rose Reisman's Enlightened Home Cooking

3. In the same saucepan, heat remaining 1 tsp (5 mL) oil over medium heat; add garlic, mushrooms, leeks, carrots, green peppers, zucchini and pearl onions. Cook for 8 to 10 minutes or until softened and browned, stirring occasionally. Stir in tomato paste and wine. Return lamb to the saucepan along with tomatoes, beef stock, rosemary and bay leaf. Bring to a boil, cover, reduce heat to medium–low, and simmer for 25 minutes or until carrots and meat are tender.

4. Meanwhile, put potatoes in a saucepan with water to cover; bring to a boil and cook for 15 minutes or until tender when pierced with the tip of a knife. In a non-stick skillet, melt margarine over medium heat; add garlic and onions and cook for 4 minutes or until softened. Drain cooked potatoes and mash with chicken stock and sour cream. Stir in onion mixture and pepper. Place potato mixture on a large serving platter and pour the stew over top.

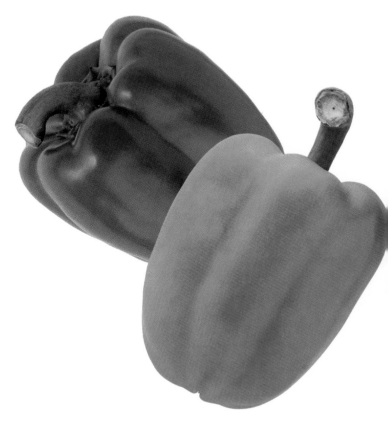

Spicy Lamb Stew

Serves 6

Sometimes you crave a dish that explodes with spicy flavors. The ginger and hot red pepper flakes used here will satisfy that craving — and soothe your soul, too. I like to serve this spice-infused stew with basmati rice.

TIP

How to cook basmati rice: Rinse 1 1/2 cups (375 mL) rice in several changes of cold water. Place in bowl; add cold water to cover. Let soak for 15 minutes; drain. In a saucepan bring 2 1/4 cups (550 mL) water and 1 tbsp (15 mL) oil to a boil; add rice and 1 tsp (5 mL) salt. Return to boil, reduce heat to low and simmer, covered, for 10 minutes. Remove and let stand, covered, for 5 minutes. Uncover and fluff with a fork. Fresh coriander, also called cilantro or Chinese parsley, lasts only a few days in the fridge before it deteriorates and turns tasteless. Wash coriander well, spin dry and wrap in paper towels; store in a plastic bag in the fridge. Leave the roots on — they keep the leaves fresh.
Buy a 3-lb (1.5 kg) leg of lamb or shoulder roast to get 1 1/2 lbs (750 g) boneless lamb.

FROM
The Comfort Food Cookbook
by Johanna Burkhard

2 tbsp	vegetable oil (approximate)	25 mL
1 1/2 lbs	boneless lean lamb, cut into 1-inch (2.5 cm) cubes	750 g
1	large onion, chopped	1
2	cloves garlic, finely chopped	2
1 tbsp	minced ginger root	15 mL
1 tsp	ground cumin	5 mL
1 tsp	ground coriander	5 mL
1/2 tsp	cinnamon	2 mL
1/2 tsp	salt	2 mL
1/4 tsp	red pepper flakes (or more, to taste)	1 mL
Pinch	ground cloves	Pinch
1 tbsp	all-purpose flour	15 mL
1/2 cup	plain yogurt	125 mL
1	large tomato, chopped	1
1/2 cup	lamb stock *or* chicken stock	125 mL
1/4 cup	chopped fresh coriander *or* parsley	50 mL

1. In a large saucepan, heat 1 tbsp (15 mL) of the oil over medium-high heat; cook lamb in batches, adding more oil as needed, until browned on all sides. Remove from pan and set aside.

2. Reduce heat to medium. Add onions, garlic, ginger root, cumin, coriander, cinnamon, salt, red pepper flakes and cloves; cook, stirring, for 2 minutes or until softened.

3. Sprinkle with flour; stir in yogurt. Cook for 1 minute or until thickened. Add lamb with any accumulated juices, tomato and stock; bring to a boil. Reduce heat and simmer, covered, for 45 minutes or until lamb is tender. Sprinkle with coriander or parsley before serving.

Serves 6 to 8

Roasted Leg of Lamb with Crunchy Garlic Topping

TIP

If you suspect the lamb will be tough, marinate it in milk, turning occasionally, for at least 3 hours before baking.

MAKE AHEAD

Prepare topping up to a day before. Pat on meat prior to baking.

PREHEAT OVEN TO 375° F (190° C)

1 tbsp	margarine	15 mL
2 tsp	crushed garlic	10 mL
1/3 cup	finely chopped onion	75 mL
1/2 cup	dry bread crumbs	125 mL
1/4 cup	crushed bran cereal★	50 mL
1/4 cup	chopped fresh parsley	50 mL
1/3 cup	chicken stock	75 mL
1	leg of lamb (2 1/2 to 3 lb [1.25 to 1.5 kg]), deboned	1
1/3 cup	red wine	75 mL
1/3 cup	beef stock	75 mL

★ *Use a wheat bran breakfast cereal*

1. In a large nonstick skillet, melt margarine; sauté garlic and onion until softened. Add bread crumbs, cereal, parsley and chicken stock; mix until well combined. If too dry, add more chicken stock.

2. Place lamb in a roasting pan and pat bread crumb mixture over top. Pour wine and beef stock into the pan. Cover and bake for 20 minutes. Uncover and bake for 15 to 20 minutes or until meat thermometer registers 140° F (60° C) for rare or until desired doneness. Serve with pan juices.

FROM
Rose Reisman Brings Home Light Cooking

Greek Baked Stuffed Potatoes with Tomatoes, Olives and Cheese

Serves 6

TIP

Use plum tomatoes if available — they have less liquid. Or you can remove the seeds from regular tomatoes.

If in a hurry, microwave potatoes. Each potato cooks in approximately 8 minutes at high power. Goat cheese or another sharp cheese can replace feta.

MAKE AHEAD

Prepare entire filling and stuff potatoes early in the day. Bake an extra 5 minutes or until hot.

PREHEAT OVEN TO 425° F (220° C)

3	medium baking potatoes	3
2 tsp	vegetable oil	10 mL
1 1/2 tsp	minced garlic	7 mL
2/3 cup	chopped green peppers	150 mL
1/2 cup	chopped red onions	125 mL
1 1/2 tsp	dried oregano	7 mL
2/3 cup	chopped fresh tomatoes	150 mL
1/3 cup	sliced black olives	75 mL
1/4 cup	chopped green onions (about 2 medium)	50 mL
1/4 cup	2% yogurt	50 mL
1/4 cup	2% milk	50 mL
1 1/2 oz	feta cheese, crumbled	40 g

1. Bake the potatoes for 45 minutes to 1 hour, or until easily pierced with the tip of a sharp knife.

2. Meanwhile, in a nonstick skillet, heat oil over medium heat. Add garlic, green peppers, red onions and oregano and cook for 7 minutes or until softened, stirring occasionally. Stir in tomatoes, black olives and green onions and cook 1 minute more. Remove from heat.

3. When potatoes are cool enough to handle, cut in half lengthwise and scoop out flesh, leaving shells intact. Place shells on baking sheet. Mash potato and add yogurt, milk and 1 oz (25 g) of the feta. Stir in vegetable mixture. Divide among potato skin shells, sprinkle with remaining feta and bake for 15 minutes, or until heated through.

FROM
Rose Reisman's Enlightened Home Cooking

Serves 4

This "fusion" recipe combines condiments from a Mongolian lamb fire-pot-dinner with western herbs and French cooking techniques. We've used a dark sesame paste, which is available in Asian markets, but if you can't find it, light sesame paste or tahini from the Greek or Mediterranean section of your supermarket makes a satisfactory substitute.

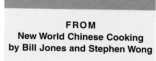

FROM
New World Chinese Cooking
by Bill Jones and Stephen Wong

Western-Style Mongolian Lamb Chops

PREHEAT OVEN TO 400° F (200° C)
OVENPROOF SKILLET OR SHALLOW ROASTING PAN

Marinade

1 tbsp	finely chopped thyme	15 mL
1 tbsp	finely chopped rosemary	15 mL
2	cloves garlic, minced	2
1/4 tsp	salt	1 mL
1/4 tsp	freshly ground black pepper	1 mL
1 tbsp	olive oil	15 mL
12	lamb chops, about 3/4 inch (2 cm) thick, trimmed	12

Sauce

1 cup	red wine	250 mL
2 tbsp	oyster sauce	25 mL
1 tbsp	hoisin sauce	15 mL
1 tbsp	chili bean sauce (or to taste)	15 mL
1 tbsp	dark sesame paste *or* tahini	15 mL

1. In a small bowl, combine ingredients for marinade; mix well. Rub marinade on the chops and set aside to marinate in the refrigerator for 2 hours or overnight.

2. Heat a large skillet, preferably ovenproof, over medium-high heat. Sear lamb chops until golden brown, for about 1 minute per side. Place in preheated oven and cook for 10 minutes. (If you don't have an ovenproof skillet, set aside skillet in which the chops were seared and transfer meat to a shallow roasting pan; when lamb is cooked, pour accumulated juices into the skillet and proceed with the recipe.) Transfer meat to a warm platter and allow to rest while finishing preparation of the sauce.

3. Add wine to skillet and cook over high heat until reduced by half. Strain through a fine sieve into a small saucepan. Add oyster sauce, hoisin sauce, chili bean sauce and sesame paste; stir to mix and heat through. Pour over lamb chops and serve.

Bok choy, a juicy and refreshing Chinese white cabbage, is also packed with vitamins and nutrients. For additional flavor, cook this dish in the same pan in which your meat has been cooked.

Pan-Fried Baby Bok Choy with Sesame Oil and Ginger

1 lb	baby bok choy	500 g
1 tbsp	vegetable oil	15 mL
1 tbsp	minced ginger root	15 mL
3 tbsp	water *or* chicken stock	45 mL
1 tsp	sesame oil	5 mL
	Salt and pepper to taste	

1. With a heavy knife, cut bok choy across the bottom to separate stems. Cut each stem in half lengthwise and wash thoroughly.

2. In a nonstick pan, heat oil for 30 seconds. Add ginger root and sauté until fragrant, for about 1 minute. Add the bok choy and cook until it begins to color and the leaves turn bright green, for about 2 to 3 minutes. Add water or stock and sesame oil; cook until all the liquid has evaporated.

3. Transfer to a platter, season with salt and pepper and serve immediately.

FROM
New World Chinese Cooking
by Bill Jones and Stephen Wong

Lamb Kebabs with Pecan Oriental Sauce

START BARBECUE OR PREHEAT BROILER

1/4 cup	chopped pecans	50 mL
2 tbsp	water	25 mL
2 tbsp	brown sugar	25 mL
2 tbsp	lemon juice	25 mL
1 tbsp	soya sauce	15 mL
1 tbsp	vegetable oil	15 mL
2 tsp	sesame oil	10 mL
1 tsp	minced ginger root	5 mL
1 tsp	minced garlic	5 mL
12 oz	boneless lamb leg, cut into 3/4-inch (2 cm) cubes	375 g
1	red or green pepper, cut into 16 chunks	1
1	red onion, cut into 16 chunks	1
1 1/2 cups	snow peas	375 mL

1. Put pecans, water, brown sugar, lemon juice, soya sauce, vegetable and sesame oils, ginger and garlic in food processor; process until smooth. Pour half of the sauce over lamb cubes and let marinate for 20 minutes or longer. Set aside the other half of the sauce.

2. Alternately thread lamb, sweet pepper chunks, onion chunks, and snow peas equally on 4 large or 8 small skewers. Barbecue for approximately 15 minutes, turning once or until lamb is medium rare (or desired level of doneness), basting with marinade sauce. Serve with remaining sauce.

Index

More of your favorite recipes

Robert Rose's Favorite
MEALS IN MINUTES

RECIPES SELECTED FROM BYRON AYANOGLU • JOHANNA BURKHARD • ANDREW CHASE
CINDA CHAVICH • BILL JONES • ROSE REISMAN • KATHLEEN SLOAN • STEPHEN WONG

ISBN 0-7788-0008-3

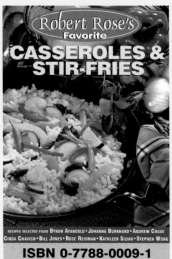

Robert Rose's Favorite
CASSEROLES & STIR-FRIES

RECIPES SELECTED FROM BYRON AYANOGLU • JOHANNA BURKHARD • ANDREW CHASE
CINDA CHAVICH • BILL JONES • ROSE REISMAN • KATHLEEN SLOAN • STEPHEN WONG

ISBN 0-7788-0009-1

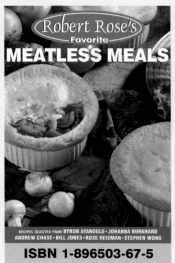

Robert Rose's Favorite
MEATLESS MEALS

RECIPES SELECTED FROM BYRON AYANOGLU • JOHANNA BURKHARD
ANDREW CHASE • BILL JONES • ROSE REISMAN • STEPHEN WONG

ISBN 1-896503-67-5

Robert Rose's Favorite
PASTA

RECIPES SELECTED FROM BYRON AYANOGLU • JOHANNA BURKHARD
ANDREW CHASE • BILL JONES • ROSE REISMAN • STEPHEN WONG

ISBN 1-896503-74-8

Robert Rose's Favorite
LIGHT DESSERTS

ISBN 1-896503-72-1

Robert Rose's Favorite
COOKIES CAKES & PIES

RECIPES SELECTED FROM BYRON AYANOGLU • JOHANNA BURKHARD
ANDREW CHASE • BILL JONES • ROSE REISMAN • STEPHEN WONG

ISBN 1-896503-71-3

Robert Rose's Favorite
SNACKS • SALADS & APPETIZERS

RECIPES SELECTED FROM BYRON AYANOGLU • JOHANNA BURKHARD
ANDREW CHASE • BILL JONES • ROSE REISMAN • STEPHEN WONG

ISBN 1-896503-51-9

Robert Rose's Favorite
SOUPS & STEWS

RECIPES SELECTED FROM BYRON AYANOGLU • JOHANNA BURKHARD
ANDREW CHASE • BILL JONES • ROSE REISMAN • STEPHEN WONG

ISBN 1-896503-69-1

Robert Rose's Favorite
CHICKEN

RECIPES SELECTED FROM BYRON AYANOGLU • JOHANNA BURKHARD
ANDREW CHASE • BILL JONES • ROSE REISMAN • STEPHEN WONG

ISBN 1-896503-53-5